Pandemic Survival Guide

Pandemic Survival Guide

Memory Verses

MPHO J. MOSIA

Foreword by Eric Bapetel

RESOURCE *Publications* • Eugene, Oregon

PANDEMIC SURVIVAL GUIDE
Memory Verses

Copyright © 2022 Mpho J. Mosia. All rights reserved. Except for brief quotations in critical publications or reviews, no part of this book may be reproduced in any manner without prior written permission from the publisher. Write: Permissions, Wipf and Stock Publishers, 199 W. 8th Ave., Suite 3, Eugene, OR 97401.

Resource Publications
An Imprint of Wipf and Stock Publishers
199 W. 8th Ave., Suite 3
Eugene, OR 97401

www.wipfandstock.com

PAPERBACK ISBN: 978-1-6667-3621-2
HARDCOVER ISBN: 978-1-6667-9424-3
EBOOK ISBN: 978-1-6667-9425-0

FEBRUARY 25, 2022 2:05 PM

Contents

Foreword by Eric Bapetel | vii

Preface | ix

Chapter 1   Only Human | 1

Chapter 2   Perfect Peace | 13

Chapter 3   Heavenly Hope | 27

Chapter 4   Purpose | 46

Chapter 5   Consuming Fire | 56

Chapter 6   Freedom | 66

Chapter 7   Good Father | 78

Chapter 8   Bountiful Soul | 89

Chapter 9   Worship | 99

Chapter 10   New Beginning | 107

Bibliography | 117

Foreword

When Mpho Mosia asked me to write the forward to her book, "Pandemic Survival Guide", I thought about the necessity of having a book on the topic in view of the recent global developments. The Covid-19 Pandemic has ravaged individuals, families, companies and nations. There's no nation or community that has not been impacted by this pandemic.

Scientists all over the world have been inundated with question after question regarding the Covid-19 virus and the proffered solutions from the scientific community in the form of the vaccine rollout. Governments have been under tremendous pressure to come up with solutions to the global pandemic that suddenly crept on all nations. The dramatic loss of lives on a global scale, disruption of all aspects of life from education, work life, economic, physical and mental health are still being assessed.

Most Christians began to look up to God in prayers for solutions. Mpho's "Pandemic Survival Guide" is a contribution from a biblical perspective. She takes the reader into different aspects of the revealed covenant names of God. Proverbs 18:10 says, "The name of the LORD is a strong fortress; the godly run to him and are safe".

As one further goes into the book, a detailed exposé of the names of God beginning with Elohim in the Preface to Jehovah Rapha, the Lord that heals in chapter one. Concluding with Jehovah Shalom, the Lord our peace, "Pandemic Survival Guide" shows the reader how to find safety in the names of God through faith and prayer.

You have not come across this book by accident. May you find in these pages the necessary guide to not only survive but to thrive in the midst of the pandemic.

Eric Bapetel
Lead Pastor, Every Nation Midrand
Johannesburg, South Africa

Preface

ELOHIM IS ONE OF the Hebrew names of God, our Creator. He's also known as *Adonai*, meaning 'The Lord' in the Hebrew language. In the Old Testament, the name *Jehovah* is most commonly used to refer to the Lord, who we now call 'our heavenly Father' under this new covenant of grace. The first record of the use of the name *Jehovah* is as part of the compound name, *Jehovah Elohim*, meaning the Lord God who created the heavens and the earth in Genesis 1, who is the Almighty One, Creator of all things, otherwise known as Yahweh.

The patriarchs of old were more acquainted with *Jehovah* as the Lord's title, this being his chosen people, the nation of Israel. However, it seems as though they might have lacked the full understanding of what the name really stood for. It was not until God spoke to Moses that the meaning of the Lord's name is recorded, when He replied to Moses saying, *"I am who I am. Say this to the people of Israel: I am has sent me to you."* (Exodus 3:14). About fourteen generations later, David saw the Lord's marvelous works in the midst of crisis and adversity, and received the revelation that, *"Those who know your name trust in you, for you, O Lord, do not abandon those who search for you."* (Psalm 9:10).

Every name of God highlights one aspect of his character, who He is, and what He is able to do. And what we believe about God will establish who we become, our morals, values and ethics, personality, and our attitudes to the life crises that the world is facing. The name *"I am"* contains each tense of the verb 'to be',

PREFACE

and could be translated, 'I was, I am, I shall always continue to be'. God revealed Himself as the self-existent, self-subsisting ever-being One to his servant Moses, who would be the first to display the righteousness and faithfulness of God to the world. All other gods are merely beings that exist. God, Yahweh is the only One who can say, "*I am*", and to the last prophet in the Old Testament, God revealed himself saying, *"I am the Lord, and I do not change."* (Malachi 3:6).

Later in the New Testament, Peter makes a declaration about Jesus, that He is indeed the Messiah, *"the Son of the living God."* (Matthew 16:16). Then once again, when Jesus was confronted by his accusers about who he really is, he simply told them, *"When you have lifted up the Son of Man on the cross, then you will understand that I am he."* (John 8:28). In disbelief they keep pressing him for a 'real' answer saying, *"You aren't even fifty years old. How can you say you have seen Abraham."* Jesus answered, *"I tell you the truth, before Abraham was even born, I am!"* (John 8:57-58).

In this book, the aim is to bring out the truth and reality of the Hebrew names of the Lord, who is Jesus Christ, and what his role is in the middle of a global pandemic, such as the one we are facing at present, COVID-19. In this modern era, where technology is right at our disposal making it easy to look up a Bible verse on Google or a Bible app, we fail to fully digest the meaning behind scripture. We've seemed to have lost touch with the integrity of the Word of God, and thus we often forget *how* to apply it to our personal circumstances because it has just become too much of a quick fix that a friend posts on social media, or a second hand message we get from a YouTube sermon. However, investing time to memorize scripture still has its place in spiritual discipline and it applies even more so today as it did many years ago in Sunday school.

Memory verses are especially critical in times of severe pressure, when there is hardly any time to pray and the whole world suddenly comes crumbling down like an avalanche right in front of you. It takes time, endurance and determination to memorize scripture. But there is still time, and there's no better time than now. Memorization increases the capacity for focus. Joshua 1:8 reminds us to, "*Study this Book of Instruction continually. Meditate on it day and night so you will be sure to obey everything written in it. Only then will you prosper and succeed in all you do.*" And sometimes the best way to truly understand something is to learn a few facts about it and have it deeply embedded in our hearts so that we will never forget it; much like the Lord's Prayer, which most of us once memorized in our very early stages of life and can still quote word for word today.

The full Bible has been translated into about 704 languages as of September 2020, with over 1,700 versions available on digital platforms. However personally, I find the New Living Translation (NLT) simple to read and understand, as it translates the entire thoughts of the original Bible text to modern everyday English. The ten memory verses in ten chapters of this book are all taken from the NLT Bible, including all the verses quoted in the text. All of these were inspired in times of deep distress. I realized that learning these verses off by heart helped me overcome most of the struggles I encountered during this trying season. I sincerely hope that these will help you too, as we all strive to survive this coronavirus pandemic and make it safe to the other side.

"But you belong to God, my dear children. You have already won a victory over those people, because the Spirit who lives in you is greater than the spirit who lives in the world."

(1 JOHN 4:4)

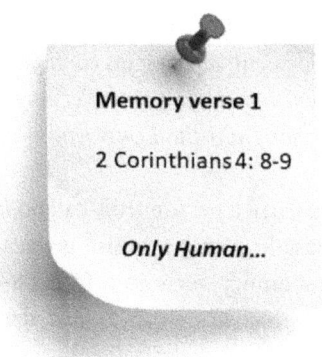

Memory verse 1

2 Corinthians 4: 8-9

Only Human...

"We are pressed on every side by troubles, but we are not crushed. We are perplexed, but not driven to despair. We are hunted down, but never abandoned by God. We get knocked down, but we are not destroyed."

-2 Corinthians 4: 8-9

Chapter 1

ONLY HUMAN

THE FIRST NAME OF God that I would like to delve into, and believe applies very much in today's coronavirus pandemic, is *Jehovah Rapha*. This is the Hebrew name for Yahweh traced back to the Old Testament, meaning "The Lord who heals". The Lord first revealed this name to his people, the Israelites after their exodus out of Egypt that was led by Moses, where he had just performed a miraculous sign of turning bitter water into potable water for the people to drink, by simply throwing in a piece of wood (Exod 15:22–25). This gesture was taken as a promise from God to his people who had borne ten plagues that He had released over all of Egypt, before being released from their oppression and slavery saying, *"If you will listen carefully to the voice of the* LORD *your God and do what is right in his sight, obeying his commands and keeping all his decrees, then I will not make you suffer any of the diseases I sent on the Egyptians; for I am the* LORD *who heals you."* (Exod 15:26).

Now the question is, can a person truly call on *Jehovah Rapha* to heal their disease based on this promise given to Israel? Can we trust that this first memory verse in 2 Cor 4:8–9 comes as a sure promise from God? That we are *not crushed,* d*riven to despair, never abandoned by God* or *not destroyed*? Can we apply it to our personal circumstances, especially right now? How can we be sure that it's true for every believer? Can we really go through trouble, fear and pain, confusion, panic attacks, disappointment, discouragement, sorrow, loss and sickness, and still be able to stand, still be able to breathe and stay alive *and* sane? How sure are we that the Lord is who He says he is, *Jehovah Rapha*? How sure are we that He will see us through this pandemic?

Well, I guess this is exactly what makes us human. We have 21 questions and even deeper concerns, we overthink things and end up doubting almost everything, even the very sure promises of our faithful God found in the Bible. Why do we panic when we go into lockdown, when alert levels and restrictions keep changing? When the very word of God is full of promises about our safety and security? Why did Thomas doubt Jesus when he saw him standing right in front of him after he'd been raised from the dead like he said he would be? And why did Peter doubt when Jesus told him to take a step out of the boat and walk on water?

Well I guess we doubt because we are all too human. Much like what Paul says in Rom 3:23, *"For everyone has sinned; we all fall short of God's glorious standard."*

A promise of healing is found in Ps 41:3 where David states it a blessing for those who are kind to the poor, that *"The Lord nurses them when they are sick and restores them to health."* Isaiah also reminds us in his prophecy about the Messiah, that he would be pierced for our rebellion, crushed for our sins, beaten so we would be made whole, and whipped so that we would be healed (Isa 53:5). And so, we know from this that Jesus Christ has already gone through all of this pain and torture for us. All of that was for the sake of our healing. But we still fail to receive and embrace these promises, we continue to doubt and fear when we hear of a loved one testing positive for COVID-19, or we ourselves get diagnosed with some other disease or condition.

How do we get through this?

How do we overcome the doubts we have about God's Word and His promises?

Well, we just have to turn away from that, change our thinking, repent and simply believe. We've just *got to* have faith! There's no other way around it—"*And it is impossible to please God without faith. Anyone who wants to come to him must believe that God exists and that he rewards those who sincerely seek him.*" (Heb 11:6). No one can convince a person to believe in something, it is up to them to receive it and truly believe it in their heart. And only God is able to cause a person to believe, by his grace and mercy.

The Bible also tells us that *this* kind of believing or 'faith' comes by hearing the Word of God (Rom 10:17), that is, the Holy Bible-"*For we live by believing and not by seeing.*" (2 Cor 5:7). In this way, hearing what the Holy Bible has to say is the best solution to strengthen our faith in God's promises. Not only that, but to maneuver through any life situation with the same power that comes from His word. COVID-19 is no exception. In fact, the Bible gives us more than just solutions to go through this pandemic without fainting, but also keys to unlock the mysteries of the nature of our glorious God, Yahweh; what he is able to manifest in us and through us in this season, and his innumerable eternal promises to us, his chosen ones—the church of Jesus Christ, as well as those who are being saved.

It is therefore important for us to continually remind ourselves that even as the church, we *are* still only human at the end of the day. We don't have control over *everything* that goes on around us. We have no control over global pandemics or any other natural disasters . Only God does, and he never changes, like we often do—*"Jesus Christ is the same yesterday, today, and forever."* (Heb 13:8). He is the Almighty God, He is the one in control . . . and we are not. We are only but mere humans awaiting Christ's return. In this world whilst in this human form, we face a lot of things that are both good and bad. These shape our human nature. We experience joy, excitement, fun adventures and thrilling roller coasters that make us feel invincible and 'king of the world!' However, this is short-lived and only defines the moments we experience, not a fixed existential state of our emotions. When life gets tough, we go through fatigue, withdrawal, sadness, sorrow, fear, hurt, pain, and anger when we lose the blisses that get taken away from us. We run out of wine, out of energy, electricity, money and sometimes even shelter. And at times, we go through lengthy states of depression as we waste away in our pain.

We are only but human, and so it remains expected of us to go through the full human experience. As Peter's sincere warning indicates to us, *"Dear friends, I warn you as "temporary residents and foreigners" to keep away from worldly desires that wage war against your very souls."* (1 Pet 2:11–12). However some hurts we face are inevitable, and some troubles may even come when we least expect. And so our natural human instincts take over, and we find ourselves back to being human again.

But let's also be encouraged by the fact that we have the power to overcome and change our circumstances. Jesus Christ has given us power, a position of superiority over the enemy when he said, *"Look, I have given you authority over all the power of the enemy, and you can walk among snakes and scorpions and crush them. Nothing will injure you."* (Luke 10:19).

In this first memory verse, 2 Cor 4:8–9, we get to see an important aspect of being human on this earth. But before fleshing it out, let's first consider what it really means according to God's Word. The best place to start would be to first put Jesus Christ aside in these following classifications, by briefly defining his true nature as God. First of all, the Bible tells us that Jesus, who is also called Emmanuel, was not conceived naturally, but was born of a virgin, his mother Mary and conceived through the power of the

Holy Spirit (Matt 1:23). And although he appeared human while he was still here on earth, the Word of God reveals to us that not only is He the Son and the Lamb of God, but that He *is* God himself (John 1:1–3) who had to go through a human experience and die a sinner's death on the cross.

Also, the New Testament testifies about the resurrection of Christ by the power of the Holy Spirit, that he is very much alive and well (Luke 24:34). Jesus proved this to many of his disciples when he appeared to them after his death and burial in the last chapters of the four Gospels (Matt 28, Mark 16, Luke 24 and John 21); and at this present moment, he is seated in heaven at God's right hand (Mark 16:19) performing his Messianic duties as our eternal High Priest (Heb 6:20) and directing the affairs of the church, such as intercession (Heb 7:25, Rom 8:34) and preparing our new homes in heaven (John 14:2). In this instance we are fully convinced that as humans, we *surely* have not been given this huge responsibility, since we see clearly in 2 Cor 5:1 that it is Christ alone who does all the building of our heavenly homes—"... *we will have a house in heaven, an eternal body made for us by God himself and not by human hands.*" This is more than reassuring that Jesus Christ, our Lord is indeed no longer human since his ascension, but God himself. The Apostle Paul further reiterates this to the church in Philippi that,

> "*You must have the same attitude that Christ Jesus had.*
> *Though he was God,*
> *he did not think of equality with God*
> *as something to cling to.*
> *Instead, he gave up his divine privileges;*
> *he took the humble position of a slave*
> *and was born as a human being.*
> *When he appeared in human form,*
> *he humbled himself in obedience to God*
> *and died a criminal's death on a cross.*"
> **(Phil 2:5–8)**

So where does that leave us? Well, it should at least be fair enough to accept that we are only but mere men, flesh and blood made from dust, and to dust we shall return (Gen 3:19). Therefore this makes us vulnerable to anything and everything that the world could possibly throw at us—" . . . *we ourselves are like fragile clay jars containing this great treasure. This makes it clear that our great power is from God, not from ourselves.* (2 Cor 4:7).

> "*We are pressed on every side by troubles . . .*
> *We are perplexed . . .* "
> *(2 Cor 4:8)*

Paul later continues to say, "*Yes, we live under constant danger of death because we serve Jesus, so that the life of Jesus will be evident in our dying bodies.*" (2 Cor 4:11). COVID-19, without a doubt, has indeed *troubled* and *perplexed* many of us, when the first reports came in from the WHO (World Health Organization) about a cluster of pneumonia cases in Wuhan, a city in the Hubei province of China on December 31 2019. These cases were later discovered to be caused by a novel coronavirus "2019-nCoV" in January 2020. Around the same time, Thai officials reported 1 laboratory-confirmed exported case to Thailand in a Chinese traveller from Wuhan. The WHO thus declared this novel coronavirus outbreak a public health emergency of international concern; and later, a global pandemic.

This had been after reports of the rapid rates of infections that occurred outside China in March 2020. By then, about 118,000 cases had been recorded in 114,000 countries, with over 4,000 deaths, which did not at all leave the media silenced. I remember the media getting their terminology mixed up in their first reports, and it became quite puzzling for most people to understand the extent of the situation we'd been faced with. The words "pandemic" and "epidemic" were usually used interchangeably up until the WHO finally termed it a pandemic when they realized that the virus was spreading at an unusually fast rate, much like an epidemic, but more intense. In this instance, coronavirus was spreading outside China, affecting the entire country and eventually spread to more countries in the world.

In short, a pandemic is an epidemic on a global scale. To make it easier, we could think of past pandemics such as the bubonic plague, HIV/AIDS and the flu pandemic of 1968. All of these share the main features of affecting a wider geographical area, infecting a larger number of people, often being caused by a new virus or viral strain that has not been seen to circulate in people for a long time thus causing more deaths, and creating immense social disruption and economic losses. It was therefore deemed necessary for the WHO to act fast, and to declare COVID-19 to be a pandemic as this allowed public health agencies to respond much quicker to contain it.

"What on earth is going on?" rang through everybody's mind almost simultaneously, when lockdowns began being imposed in several countries around the world. These shut downs we considered to be a strategy to reduce the spread of what scientists had now called "SARS-CoV-2" (Severe acute respiratory syndrome coronavirus 2), the virus that causes COVID-19 (coronavirus disease 2019), a successor to SARS-CoV-1 that caused the 2002–2004 SARS outbreak.

On March 27 2020, South Africa started a nation-wide lockdown, following a national shut-down in Italy that was later joined by France and Spain, with Australia ordering foreign travellers to self-isolate, and with several other countries extending their entry bans to contain the virus. Earlier that month, Italy's death toll had overtaken China which consequently prompted an unprecedented state-wide "stay-at-home" order in California and business shut downs in New York. On March 24, the International Olympic Committee and Japan Prime Minister Shinzo Abe announced the postponement of the 2020 summer games, as India also decided to join the lockdown. This global chaos created panic like never seen before, with social media fanning the flames by pointing fingers at politicians, and embracing all sorts of conspiracy theories. Fear gripped almost everyone with suicide rates shooting up skyrocket, while the pandemic continued to cause more and more deaths and a severe deterioration in mental health.

"We are hunted down... We get knocked down..."
(2 Cor 4:8-9)

Whether black or white, rich or poor, slave or free, educated or not, most people in the world were, and still *are* affected by this plague. It has indeed *hunted us down* like an enemy, and put us all in a very tight spot. Our most honest and true expressions, our smiles have all been hidden behind face masks; and giving a hug to console a dejected friend has almost become obsolete and even illegal. The virus *knocked* some of us down by taking the lives of those who are dear to us, our family members, our relatives and closest friends. Plans were cancelled, weddings postponed, and attending a friend's funeral became a life-threatening risk.

The pandemic affected the entire food system with border closures, trade restrictions and confinement measures preventing farmers from accessing markets, including buying inputs and selling their produce; and agricultural workers from harvesting crops, and ultimately disrupting domestic and international food supply chains. It caused reduced access to health facilities, decimated jobs and placed millions of livelihoods in jeopardy. Many breadwinners lost their jobs and became ill, some even died. The food security of millions of lives was placed under severe threat, more especially for marginalized populations, leaving tens of millions of people at risk of falling into extreme poverty.

And even with all this in mind, the Word of God reminds us to *"Rejoice in our confident hope. Be patient in trouble, and keep on praying."* (Rom 12:12). But can one truly rejoice when the whole world's suddenly turned up-side down? Is it really possible to keep calm and be patient?

Well, this verse is worth considering when we realize that we can't solve all the world's problems. When we've run out of all options, there is simply nothing more we can do but to pray. Paul reminds us that, *"Our present troubles are small and won't last very long. Yet they produce for us a glory that vastly outweighs them and will last forever! So we don't look at the troubles we can see now; rather, we fix our gaze on things that cannot be seen. For the things* we see now will soon be gone, but the things we cannot see will last forever." (2 Cor 4:17–18). This gives us confidence that things are bound to get better, and that there is light at the end of the tunnel.

> "... But we are not crushed... not driven to despair... never abandoned by God... not destroyed."
> (2 Cor 4:8–9)

As I meditate on this memory verse, I'm vividly reminded by the song, "Amazing Grace", one of the most beloved hymns of the last two centuries, and still celebrated in many churches all over the world today. The song was referenced in Harriet Beecher Stowe's anti-slavery novel *Uncle Tom's Cabin* and received a surge of popularity during two of the nation's greatest crises: the Civil War and the Vietnam War. Ironically, this inspiring song, closely associated with the African American community, was written by a former enslaver, John Newton whose life very much mimicked the life of the Apostle Paul. The *Amazing Grace* Broadway musical tells Newton's life story from his early days as a shameless libertine in the British navy to his Christian conversion and taking up the abolitionist cause to repudiate slavery. The lyrics to the song are in fact quite amazing as the title itself suggests, and should remind us of Christ's redemptive work on the Cross of Calvary that will save us and get us through this pandemic.

This first memory verse (2 Cor 4:8–9) comes from one of the inspiring letters of the Apostle Paul, who mainly addressed the churches in Rome, Corinth, Galatia, Ephesus, Philippi, Thessalonica as well as his fellow co-workers in the ministry including Timothy, Titus and Philemon. Paul mostly dealt with ministering to the Jews and Gentiles about the Good News of Jesus Christ, and was considered to be a prolific contributor of the New Testament, having written about nearly a third of it during his missionary journeys. As a servant of Christ, who had a deep personal encounter with the Lord, Paul couldn't help but to serve God with all the strength he had, by simply responding to the Lord's amazing grace that saved him.

Though being saved by grace and having founded so many churches, bringing up several world changers in the ministry, Paul was just as human as we are. He was prone to sin and weaknesses like many of us, but a champion apostle nonetheless. What's inspiring about Paul's writings is that he was never too shy to publicly announce that he was a flawed man. This is noted in Romans 7 where he sheds light about his struggle with sin. We also come across this in his testimony about his vision and the thorn in his flesh that always pointed him back to God's amazing grace, even after having being a great carrier of so many profound revelations of Jesus-

> "If I wanted to boast, I would be no fool in doing so, because I would be telling the truth. But I won't do it, because I don't want anyone to give me credit beyond what they can see in my life or hear in my message, even though I have received such wonderful revelations from God. So to keep me from becoming proud, I was given a thorn in my flesh, a messenger from Satan to torment me and keep me from becoming proud. Three different times I begged the Lord to take it away. Each time he said, "My grace is all you need. My power works best in weakness." So now I am glad to boast about my weaknesses, so that the power of Christ can work through me. That's why I take pleasure in my weaknesses, and in the insults, hardships, persecutions, and troubles that I suffer for Christ. For when I am weak, then I am strong." (2 Cor 12:6–10)

Paul also makes us realize that being a believer doesn't mean that we have it all together or even know it *all* from the get-go. In Rom 7, Paul reveals one of his sins of the flesh, which was to covet, a sin that was explicitly forbidden in the ten commandments of the Mosaic law (Exod 20:17). Paul was well aware of his sinful nature, and he clearly acknowledged it even as he spoke to the churches, "*So the trouble is not with the law, for it is spiritual and good. The trouble is with me, for I am all too human, a slave to sin.*" (Rom 7:14).

Through Paul's honesty, we are reminded that we *are* only human, humans that have populated the earth. No wonder the earth has to go through periodic catastrophes. It is filled with sin, since we know that the devil is behind running most of the world's systems-"*Satan, who is the god of this world, has blinded the minds of those who don't believe.*" (2 Cor 4:4). Mankind instinctively has a sinful nature because of the fall of man in the Garden of Eden (Gen 3). And so Christians, believers, the church have all fallen short of God's glorious standards, and we are therefore prone to sin. However, we do differ from the world because our hearts are filled with hope in the midst of this judgment that has come upon the entire world; and this is hope lies only Jesus Christ, the hope of glory (Col 1:27). Paul also reminds us that, "*. . . this hope will not lead to disappointment. For we know how dearly God loves us, because he has given us the Holy Spirit to fill our hearts with his love.*" (Rom 5:5).

Jehovah Rapha is therefore one of the greatest names of God that we can identify our Messiah with in this present situation, because we are filled with hope and confidence that He loves us unconditionally, even in our short-comings. He is the Lord who heals us, and he is able to heal any kind of affliction that our bodies may suffer from. This is revealed in one of most famous healing stories recorded in the synoptic gospels.

> "*A woman in the crowd had suffered for twelve years with constant bleeding. She had suffered a great deal from many doctors, and over the years she had spent everything she had to pay them, but she had gotten no better. In fact, she had gotten worse. She had heard about Jesus, so she came up behind him through the crowd and touched his robe. For she thought to herself, "If I can just touch his robe, I will be healed." Immediately the bleeding stopped, and she could feel in her body that she had been healed of her terrible condition.*" (Mark 5:25-29).

In this story, we can identify *Jehovah Rapha* with healing a chronic disorder; and in many of his other miracles we see that there was no disease that was too hard for him to heal. You can name it, leprosy—an infectious and severe skin disease that causes nerve damage, Jesus was able to take it away. He could cure blindness, fever, paralysis, deafness, and even raise the dead. Surely there is no sickness that Christ cannot heal—"*What do you mean, 'If I can'?*" *Jesus asked. "Anything is possible if a person believes.*" (Mark 9:23).

> *"My thoughts are nothing like your thoughts," says the Lord. "And my ways are far beyond anything you could imagine."*
>
> (Isa 55:8)

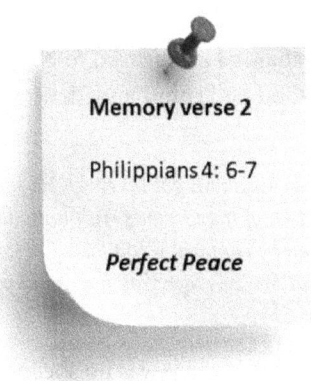

Memory verse 2

Philippians 4: 6-7

Perfect Peace

"Don't worry about anything; instead, pray about everything. Tell God what you need, and thank him for all he has done. Then you will experience God's peace, which exceeds anything we can understand. His peace will guard your hearts and minds as you live in Christ Jesus"

-Philippians 4: 6-7

Chapter 2

PERFECT PEACE

JEHOVAH JIREH MEANING "THE Lord our provider" is the Hebrew name for God that is widely recognized by the Christian community all over the world. We identify its meaning with provision, stemming from its literal translation from the book of Genesis— "*Abraham named the place Yahweh-Yireh (which means "the LORD will provide"). To this day, people still use that name as a proverb: "On the mountain of the LORD it will be provided."* (Gen

22:14). God revealed this to Abraham when He tested his faith by asking him to sacrifice his son, Isaac on a mountain in the land of Moriah. Surely, Abraham's faith proved to be true when he set out to do exactly what God had commanded, without a shadow of doubt.

> *"The next morning Abraham got up early. He saddled his donkey and took two of his servants with him, along with his son, Isaac. Then he chopped wood for a fire for a burnt offering and set out for the place God had told him about."* (Gen 22:3).

When Isaac realized that there was no sheep to be sacrificed, he asked his father what the deal was. This is where Abraham's response gave him full assurance that the Lord would indeed provide (Gen 22:8). Although not having any evidence of this, Abraham believed, despite God not having told him how it would happen. It was only when Abraham was on the verge of killing Isaac that the Lord showed him a ram caught by its horns in the thickets, which then became the substitute for his son's death on the alter (Gen 22:13). And from that day onwards, Abraham named that mountain "*Jehovah Jireh*" because of the miracle provision that he'd just witnessed from Yahweh.

This second memory verse found in Phil 4:6–7 carries a lot of weight about the responsibility of faith that the Lord has given us. From Gen 22, we see that Abraham was undeniably the father of faith, as the book of Hebrews tells us in the New Testament. If Abraham hadn't had the faith to listen and to obey the Lord's instruction, or if he'd decided to protest against the Lord about this heavy task of having to kill his beloved son of the promise, he most likely would've never found out about God's faithful ministry of providing for his people. Hebrews 11 has much to say about this and even paints an interesting image of what having faith really means; that it, *"shows us the reality of what we hope for; it is the evidence of things we cannot see."* (Heb 11:1). And certainly we do *see* that Abraham really possessed this gift of faith, when he answered Isaac's question about the sacrificial sheep.

Perfect Peace

Today as we find ourselves faced with this COVID-19 pandemic, we've had to witness a steep drop in the world economy that has raised boisterous panic in every class of society because of all the numerous business shut downs and job losses. There have been fears of global recessions since the $5 trillion wipe out from the global market in February 2020. This happened when the S&P 500 suffered its biggest weekly drop since the 2008 financial crisis. Worse yet, markets continued to fall drastically in March 2020, with the U.S. Federal reserve doing its best to curb the situation by cutting interest rates by half a percentage point, as a strategy to stem the economic damage. Around the same time, crude oil prices plunged nearly 25%, the biggest daily rout since the 1991 Gulf War, which has now led to the price war between Saudi Arabia and Russia, when Riyadh failed to persuade Moscow that deep supply cutbacks were needed to overcome the loss of demand from the pandemic. By May 2020, the U.S. economy had lost 20.5 million jobs, the steepest plunge since the Great Depression. The unemployment rate surged to 14.7%, while Avianca Holdings, Latin-America's second-largest airline was forced to file for bankruptcy, later followed by LATAM Airlines group, the continent's largest carrier.

Panic further arose when the WHO reported that coronavirus could be endemic, like HIV/AIDS, and would never go away. This led to serious warnings from the United Nations about a looming mental illness crisis, as millions of people were surrounded by death and disease and forced into isolation, poverty and extreme anxiety. Clearly there was more than enough room to worry, not only with the news feeds that we were being bombarded with on a daily basis, but the idea that some of what we were getting wasn't even true, but 'fake news'. It made it maddening to have to filter out facts from the conspiracies, and by and large forced many people to go into severe depression when all the hope in the world seemed to have been lost.

> *"Don't worry about anything; instead, pray about everything..."*
> *(Phil 4:6)*

This second memory verse begins with a comforting instruction from the Apostle Paul, whose letter to the church of Philippi was written during his incarceration after visiting Greece and his second missionary visit journey back from Antioch, where he and his companion, Silas had been accused of disturbing the city. They'd been subject to much ridicule and torment, having been stripped, beaten with wooden rods and thrown into prison (Acts 16:20–23). In this letter, there is a sense that Paul was deeply sad and troubled, almost as if he wished to die because of the immense hostility he'd endured during his journey of spreading the Gospel (Phil 1:21). Later in the epistle, after having evaluated his walk with the Lord and what it had produced in him, he gradually became filled with joy (Phil 4:4), causing him to encourage the other believers not to worry about anything, but to pray instead, adding to Peter's words, *"Give all your worries and cares to God, for he cares about you."* (1 Pet 5:7).

Much like Paul's distressing experiences, the coronavirus pandemic has left millions of lives in despair and depression. There've been immense retrenchments, commotions in homes and workplaces during lockdowns, deaths lurking about in our churches and families, wars and threats of wars in political systems, and fear gripping the lowliest of people who aren't even exposed to the western world.

It is without a doubt that prayer had to be and should be the central goal in every person's life during this global tribulation. But how do we press into prayer in the midst of great distress and melancholy?

In a general sense, we can regard prayer as a solemn request for help or an expression of thanksgiving addressed to God. In the most troubling of situations, we see that several prominent figures in the Bible knew much about the power of prayer and the wonderful results it produces. Dating back to the Old Testament, we see that Hannah's deep anguish to conceive a child led her to pray in her most sincere state of misery (1 Sam 1:1–10). Hannah showed to have total reliance on God to provide for her when there was no other option but to pray in her situation, which ultimately drove her to even make a serious vow to dedicate the child to the Lord as an expression of her intense desperation.

King David, who would later be anointed by Hannah's son, Samuel, also showed to be a prayer warrior. We read most of his prayers in the book of Psalm, where he asked for ...

- The Lord's forgiveness (after having sinned with Bathsheba)— *"For the honor of your name, O Lord, forgive my many, many sins."* (Ps 25:11);
- To stay in the Lord's presence forever—*"The one thing I ask of the Lord—the thing I seek most—is to live in the house of the Lord all the days of my life, delighting in the Lord's perfections and meditating in his Temple."* (Ps 27:4);
- The Lord's continued mercy through all the great difficulties he faced—*"Remember, O Lord, your compassion and unfailing love, which you have shown from long ages past."* (Ps 25:6);
- Deliverance from his enemies (Ps 109);
- The Lord's guidance—*"Show me the right path, O Lord; point out the road for me to follow."* (Ps 25:4).

During Israel's return from the Babylonian exile, we also come across a righteous man named Ezra, who demonstrated his robust confidence in the power of prayer. Not only that, but he realized that some tasks, such as the return to Israel's native land after captivity would take more than just prayer to make it through a safe journey:

> *"So we fasted and earnestly prayed that our God would take care of us, and he heard our prayer."*(Ezra 8:23).

From this, we see that fasting is a critical step to receiving effective deliverance and breakthrough. It is often the best way to humble ourselves and to earnestly seek the heart of God for any given situation or task that may seem difficult or even impossible. We see that when Jesus' disciples tried to cast out an evil-spirit from a demon-possessed boy who suffered from seizures that often threw him into the fire or water, they failed to deliver him. This was mainly due to their 'lack of faith' as Jesus pointed out (Matt 17:20). They had to do better than that. Jesus revealed a key to breakthrough and told them that, *"This kind does not go out except by prayer and fasting."* (Matt 17:21, King James Version). Jesus undeniably acknowledged the power of fasting, and he was faithful enough to validate this key to his disciples because he himself had experienced its operative value in the wilderness before he began his ministry (Matt 4:1–11).

Fasting isn't a spiritual duty that demonstrates a sacrifice to God, as some people in the Old Testament might have taken it (Isa 58); and it has very little to do with "suffering for Christ", but rather, for our own growth benefit. Depriving ourselves of food and drink for a period of time makes room for God to speak, by clearing out all the junk that regularly consumes our minds, like indigestion issues we might experience after having a big meal. Fasting offers physical *and* spiritual benefits that cleanse the body and the soul, in that when we intentionally set aside a time to fast, we know that it also means a time for prayer. This causes us to spend much more time in the presence of God than usual. By doing this, we experience a supernatural elevation of faith as we draw closer to him. James 4:8 says, *"Come close to God, and God will come close to you. Wash your hands, you sinners; purify your hearts, for your loyalty is divided between God and the world."* Therefore, we find ourselves shifting our focus away from fleshly desires that consume our time and energy, and replace it with God's Word. This ultimately produces wonderful results, breakthroughs, miracles, strength and improves our faith and trust in God.

"Tell God what you need . . . "
(Phil 4:6)

Another great example of powerful prayer can be seen in the life of Jabez, who was more honorable than all of his brothers, but ironically received his name from a painful birth. However, Jabez did not let his name define his identity. He went against the odds of having a hopeless name and dysfunctional beginning, to becoming a man who firmly stood on the power of fervent prayer. He cried out to the Lord with confidence and boldness and made one of the most remarkable, and yet simple prayers in the Bible—"*Oh, that you would bless me and expand my territory! Please be with me in all that I do, and keep me from all trouble and pain!*" And God granted him his request." (1 Chr 9:10).

The Old Testament is quite clear on the powerful effects that a simple prayer has, and that God answers our prayers in whatever state we find ourselves in, whether in deep sin or in our most consecrated state. Prayer is therefore a curative key for any kind of trouble we face. It is a gateway to all the solutions to our problems, no matter how awful they may be.

In the New Testament, Paul points out a significant ministry of the Holy Spirit that comes in handy when we don't know *how* or *what* to pray for, where we sometimes find ourselves in pressing circumstances that are just way beyond our control. Like the unexplainable mental disorders resulting from this pandemic, which seem to have debilitated people's cognizance of their surroundings or cause some form of severe anxiety or mental paralysis, where many were reported to have lost their minds completely. It may even be all the more harder to pray objectively when one finds themselves in that kind of state, where it becomes challenging to even tell what's real versus what isn't. The causes to these types of mental breakdowns could in part be as a result of the lockdowns and self-isolation impositions, which makes sense in that, they *have* really made it difficult for people to establish or maintain their true relationships, since some can only be supported by physical means.

Quarantines have especially made it almost impossible to express our real emotions to the next best person who could point us in the right direction, and this has led to most people not even receiving the kind of help they need. For instance, reaching out to the local pastor for a healing prayer, as Jas 5:14 says, "*You should call for the elders of the church to come and pray over you, anointing you with oil in the name of the Lord.*" This may not always be as easy as it sounds, especially when logistics becomes a factor, and the shutting down of churches only seemed to have worsened things for the sick and tormented who found themselves not having direct access to the church elders or their pastors for prayer and counseling. However regardless of this, the Word of God reminds us that, *"The Lord is good, a strong refuge when trouble comes. He is close to those who trust in him."* (Nah 1:7).

Either way, in such cases, we may find ourselves worn down and a little less hopeful. And the only best thing we can do is to encourage ourselves in prayer, sometimes without knowing where or *how* to start our conversation with God. Paul reminds us that, *"And the Holy Spirit helps us in our weakness. For example, we don't know what God wants us to pray for. But the Holy Spirit prays for us with groanings that cannot be expressed in words."* (Rom 8:26). This is where praying in tongues comes in, a precious gift of the Holy Spirit. Paul said, *"For if I pray in tongues, my spirit is praying, but I don't understand what I am saying. Well then, what shall I do? I will pray in the spirit, and I will also pray in words I understand. I will sing in the spirit, and I will also sing in words I understand."* (1 Cor 14:14–15). He understood that praying this way strengthens a person's spirit and eventually charges them up to pray God's will over their life and their situation. He further urged the church in Ephesus to, *"Pray in the Spirit at all times and on every occasion."* (Eph 6:18); and often times, to receive a breakthrough, persistence is key.

"One day Jesus told his disciples a story to show that they should always pray and never give up . . . " (Luke 18:1–8). The opening of this parable given by Jesus to his disciples makes the story very clear from the get go. It's a story about a widow who repeatedly pleaded with an unrighteous judge in a certain city to render her justice in a dispute she had with an adversary. Here, Jesus does not state how many times this woman kept going back and forth to the judge for this, but he does make it clear that this man neither feared God nor cared for people, and so to convince him to even consider the thought of helping this helpless widow in any way would seem almost impossible. What's striking about this parable is that the widow unquestionably believed in the power of persistence. Taking "no" for an answer wasn't something she was accustomed to. She could've put her faith in the justice system that probably came from her past experiences, so much so that she understood that her case qualified for a review by this unjust man. She knew that her persistence in this matter would trigger some kind of response, a change in response, or any other kind of response that would eventually come down to a complete change of mind and cause justice to triumph. In this parable, the woman had a goal, she wanted to resolve the issue that she had with her opponent, and so she took the right steps of presenting her case to the judge, persistently so.

In many instances, we fall into the temptation of giving up on the things we've set out to do when we go through a delay, because we simply get discouraged along the way. We get turned down, we get pushed back, we get awkward looks, and the door just keeps getting slammed back right into our faces. And so we grow weary of going back only to get the same response. But here, Jesus gives an important key to effective prayer: not to give up but to keep pressing forward. Praying faithfully and persistently not only keeps us motivated and focused towards our goals, but provides a stage to ingeniously learn the ways of God, which draws us closer to him. And this could sometimes be through simple trial and error. It reveals more about the character of God that our minds would've never conceived than if we'd chosen to give up in our first attempt. Persistent prayer also has the power to open doors to understanding God's view of the world around us. By praying about something repeatedly, God is faithful to guide and lead us towards unlocking mysteries of possible reasons that could otherwise contributed to our prayers being delayed.

The Lord revealed something quite profound to the Prophet Daniel that point to one of the reasons why some of our prayers may be hindered. But it all had to start somewhere. Daniel 9 shows that he first had to humble himself by fasting and praying for the forgiveness of *his* sins, and the sins of his people that he came across in the writings of the Prophet Jeremiah. This was probably Daniel's first encounter with the real causes for his people's captivity. And so he had to prepare his heart to receive understanding from the Lord about what the exile meant for the nation of Israel and what Jeremiah's prophecies meant about the coming disaster and the fate of his people. David writes in Ps 66:18 that if he had not confessed the sin in his heart, the Lord would not have listened. And sometimes all it takes to receive a breakthrough starts by simply confessing our sins to the Lord to clear our conscience— *"And since we have a great High Priest who rules over God's house, let us go right into the presence of God with sincere hearts fully trusting him. For our guilty consciences have been sprinkled with Christ's blood to make us clean, and our bodies have been washed with pure water."* (Heb 10:21–22). We see that as Daniel continued to pray, fast and confess his sins for 21 days, a miraculous answer appeared through the angel, Gabriel who presented him with more insight about what he'd just read in the scriptures (Dan 9:20). Daniel further received another vision from a different angel of the Lord who revealed an important message for him explaining the delay of his prayer:

> *"Don't be afraid, Daniel. Since the first day you began to pray for understanding and to humble yourself before your God, your request has been heard in heaven. I have come in answer to your prayer. But for twenty-one days the spirit prince of the kingdom of Persia blocked my way. Then Michael, one of the archangels, came to help me, and I left him there with the spirit prince of the kingdom of Persia."* (Dan 9:12–13).

From his message we see that there's a spiritual warfare in the unseen world, where angels are constantly fighting against demons to deliver God's answers to our prayers. Unfortunately, this is not always evident to our natural senses; we simply don't always know what's taking so long. Nevertheless, Jesus made his strong point that persistence is key, endurance is vital, and that we should never give up on our prayers. The Apostle Paul also reminds us that we should always be on guard while we pray and seek the Lord—*"For we are not fighting against flesh-and-blood enemies, but against evil rulers and authorities of the unseen world, against mighty powers in this dark world, and against evil spirits in the heavenly places."* (Eph

6:12). And so the answers may not always come straight away for some of our prayers. It seems that from this story that Jesus told, praying persistently leads to understanding of God's ways and his will for our lives, which in the case of the widow, is justice and ultimate victory.

In this second memory verse, Paul urges us to present our needs and petitions to God, to make our requests known to Him so that our prayers are guided and purposeful, well despite the fact that God already knows what we need before we even ask him (Matt 6:8). Nonetheless, it's always good to let Him know, because conversing with the Lord in prayer is also a form of communion. It's fellowship with Him, and so it's not a bad thing to chat about our needs and concerns with our Father, who is also our friend. Jesus Christ taught his disciples to pray this way—"*Give us today the food we need and forgive us our sins, as we have forgiven those who sin against us. And don't let us yield to temptation, but rescue us from the evil one.*" (Matt 6:9–13). We all have different needs and desires that God has placed in our hearts and at times, this list could go on forever. But what's really great about prayer, is that there is no limit. We could go on for days listing all the things we want because our heavenly Father loves us and wants to give us our heart's desires, generously—"*You haven't done this before. Ask, using my name, and you will receive, and you will have abundant joy.*" (John 16:24).

Right now it seems what most people really want from God is for things on this planet to be restored back to order, for coronavirus to be fully eradicated and perhaps, world peace? But can the world truly be at peace when we have so many divided beliefs? And, how long will it be until the virus completely goes away? That's if it ever does.

But thankfully, in his mercy the Lord gave us a special promise that, "*If my people who are called by my name will humble themselves and pray and seek my face and turn from their wicked ways, I will hear from heaven and will forgive their sins and restore their land.*" (2 Chr 7:14). He *is* the Lord who provides at the end of the day, *Jehovah Jireh,* and so there is nothing He cannot do—"*I am the Lord, the God of all the peoples of the world. Is anything too hard for me?"* (Jer 32:27). Jesus says these words in Matt 7:7-8, *"Keep on asking, and you will receive what you ask for. Keep on seeking, and you will find. Keep on knocking, and the door will be opened to you. For everyone who asks, receives. Everyone who seeks, finds. And to everyone who knocks, the door will be opened."*

> *". . . and thank him for all he has done."*
> *(Phil 4:6)*

By his grace, the Lord has been faithful to carry us through this pandemic right up until now. He continues to be the sustainer of our lives, our inheritance and our cup of blessing (Ps 16:5). Surely there's much more we can think of to justify our praises and thankfulness toward Him. And so as we continue to ask, we need to approach him with a sincere heart of gratitude.

For instance, your heartbeat and the breath in your lungs are the most vital things at this very moment. Without them, you wouldn't have the ability to perceive or focus your attention while running your eyes through this text. One of the reasons why the Bible stimulates our desire to praise the Lord is simply because of all the things He has done for us and given to us, one of them being the gift of life. David praised the Lord in his time of crisis saying, *"I will bless the Lord who guides me; even at night my heart instructs me. I know the Lord is always with me. I will not be shaken, for he is right beside me."* (Ps 16:7-8). Here, David points out that the Lord's protection over our lives is one of the reasons to be grateful for—*"In peace I will lie down and sleep, for you alone, O Lord, will keep me safe."* (Ps 4:8).

It's also necessary to consider all the people that God has placed in our lives. This includes our friends and family, our pastors and leaders, our next door neighbors who are probably prayer warriors, interceding for us each and every single day without us even knowing it. The prayers and petitions that *you* have laid before God are all good and well, but God also uses those around us to pray for us. Paul tells his spiritual son, Timothy that, *"I urge you, first of all, to pray for all people. Ask God to help them; intercede* on their behalf, and give thanks for them. Pray this way for kings and all who are in authority so that we can live peaceful and quiet lives marked by godliness and dignity. This is good and pleases God our Savior, who wants everyone to be saved and to understand the truth." (1 Tim 2:1–4). Surely from this, we see that it pleases God when we stand in the gap and pray for others, including those in authority, our leaders. It also pleases Him when we pray for those who are lost to come to repentance and be saved.

Just a couple of weeks before the coronavirus pandemic shut down in the U.S., Kari Jobe, an American contemporary Christian music singer and songwriter held a songwriting session with her husband, Cody Carnes and Elevation Worship's Steven Furtick and Chris Brown. Its words are directly inspired by Bible passages from the books of Numbers and Psalms. They penned the tune in a writing session in February 2020, at Charlotte, North Carolina prior to premiering it at the church's Sunday service on March 2020. The song originated with Furtick singing Moses' priestly blessing from Num 6:24–26.

> "May the Lord bless you and protect you.
> May the Lord smile on you and be gracious to you.
> May the Lord show you his favor and give you his peace."

This song has certainly touched and comforted many souls all around the world and has made a huge impact in families that have been and *still are* going through this crisis. The song will continue to do so for perhaps, future pandemics? Since it reminds us of how we ought to continue to love and bless one another in the midst of trials and adversity.

> "Then you will experience God's peace, which exceeds anything we can understand. His peace will guard your hearts and minds as you live in Christ Jesus."
> (Phil 4:7)

Peace is always good, but peace beyond measure is even better. Peace is the heartwarming reassurance that everything will be alright, and that we are, and *will be* saved from God's coming wrath upon the world. Peace is quietness, stillness and tranquility in a world gone crazy, and knowing that Jesus Christ is with us through the storm. In this memory verse, Paul speaks of God's peace that exceeds anything we can understand. How could we possibly imagine what this kind of peace feels like? Since all we can imagine right now is the total obliteration of this pandemic. But in this verse, it seems that Paul had something *way* better in mind. The prophet Isaiah prophesied this message about Judah's future- *"And this righteousness will bring peace. Yes, it will bring quietness and confidence forever."* (Isa 32:17). This promise has partially been fulfilled by Jesus before his crucifixion that, *"I am leaving you with a gift—peace of mind and heart. And the peace I give is a gift the world cannot give. So don't be troubled or afraid."* (John 14:27). He showed this to be possible when he calmed the storm at sea (Mark 4:35-41), and we hear it in the song that Chandler Moore performed with Justin Bieber, "Jireh" that in all things, God's abiding presence is more than enough.

> *"You will keep in perfect peace all who trust in you, all whose thoughts are fixed on you!"*
>
> (Isa 26:3)

"But we are citizens of heaven, where the Lord Jesus Christ lives. And we are eagerly waiting for him to return as our Savior."

-Philippians 3: 20

Chapter 3

HEAVENLY HOPE

JEHOVAH TSIDKENU MEANING, "THE Lord is our Righteousness" is the Hebrew name for God taken from the book of Jeremiah, where Yahweh had promised Israel's returning exiles that the Messiah would come from the line of David- *"And this will be his name: The Lord Is Our Righteousness.' In that day, Judah will be saved, and Israel will live in safety."* (Jer 23:6). This confirmed Nathan's prophecy to King David in 2 Sam 7:12–13- *"For when you die and are buried with your ancestors, I will raise up one of your descendants, your own offspring, and I will make his kingdom strong. He is the one who will build a house—a temple—for my name. And I will secure his royal throne forever."*

Jeremiah further reiterated this prophecy that the 'Branch of righteousness' would indeed come from the line of David, and not from the royal line of Jeconiah, the cursed and last king of Judah (Jer 22:30). This would therefore have to be through Nathan's descendants, one of David's other sons that the Messiah would rule as king of the Jews from David's throne (Luke 3:31).

> "*It seemed as if the royal line of David was cut down like a tree and only a stump remained. Yet God would take that stump and bring forth a green shoot, a Branch. This 'Branch of righteousness', Jesus Christ our Messiah would lead God's people as a successful King for all eternity. Prosperity, justice, and righteousness would mark His reign and his reign would extend to the earth, not only the boundaries of Israel.*" [1]

"But we are citizens of heaven . . . "
(Phil 3:20)

Jeremiah announced that *Jehovah Tsidkenu* would be the name by which our Messiah will be called. He will be the way that the righteousness of Yahweh is given to His people, so that He himself is *our* righteousness. Paul may have had this same promise in mind when he said, "*This Good News tells us how God makes us right in his sight. This is accomplished from start to finish by faith. As the Scriptures say, "It is through faith that a righteous person has life.*" (Rom 1:17). And we know that we are only made right in God's sight by believing in Jesus, our Messiah. In this way, God's gift of righteousness, much like the gift of faith that God has freely given us has made a way for us to be united with his Son (1 Cor 1:30), which brings us right to the fullness of our third memory verse, Phil 3:20, that we are indeed citizens of heaven, and not of this earth because of the unity we have with God's Son. We see that Paul confirms this in his letter to the church in Ephesus where he said, "*For he raised us from the dead along with Christ and seated us*

---

1. Guzik, *Enduring Word Bible Commentary*

with him in the heavenly realms because we are united with Christ Jesus." (Eph 2:6) and, "So now you Gentiles are no longer strangers and foreigners. You are citizens along with all of God's holy people. You are members of God's family." (Eph 2:19).

On February 5 2020, still in the early days of the coronavirus outbreak, alarming news from Japan reported that 3,700 passengers had to be quarantined aboard the Diamond Princess, a Carnival Corp cruise liner, where more than 700 passengers tested positive for COVID-19 and 14 died. The quarantine lasted nearly a month. Ten days after news from Japan, the death of a Chinese tourist hospitalized in France was reported to be the first fatality reported in Europe. By 26 February, the number of new infections inside China had been overtaken by those elsewhere for the first time, with Italy and Iran emerging as new epicenters. By 10 April global deaths had reached 100,000 and spiked up to 500,000 with confirmed cases topping 10 million by 28 April. By the month of September 2020 death rates went beyond a million, with coronavirus-related illnesses having doubled from half a million in just three months led by fatalities in the U.S., Brazil and India. These spikes led to Britain telling its people to work from home, and bars and restaurants having to close up early.

Since then, national lockdown restrictions have continued to go through changes and several adjustments to suit the citizens of different countries in order to 'flatten the curve', usually stemming from statistical reports of new infections, death rates and the country's population size.

For example, in South Africa, where the current population is approximately 60 million people in nine different provinces with diverse cultures, ethnicities and languages, core lockdown regulations were first put in place in March 2020 by the South African government. These were followed by updates from President Cyril Ramaphosa who held regular televised 'family meeting' to communicate important messages about changes to alert levels (1 to 5 being the most stringent measures). On June 27 2021, after seeing a steep rise in infection and death rates, with close to 60,000 deaths recorded since the start of the pandemic, the president once again gave a report on the adjustment of alert level 4 (from level 3), which had mainly been triggered by reports of a new Delta variant of the coronavirus disease. In his report, he highlighted the following about the adjusted alert level 4 restrictions from the presidential cabinet:

- The coronavirus is mutating and creating new variants (Beta variant in 2020 and now Delta variant first discovered in India, detected in five provinces of South Africa)
- The new variant is rapid and more transmissible variant through person-to-person contact
- Emerging scientific evidence suggests that people previously infected with the Beta variant may not have full protection against the new Delta variant and could get re-infected
- Preliminary data from other countries suggest that infections and clinical illness in children are more common with the new Delta variant
- Seven-day average of new daily cases has overtaken the peak of the first wave (July 2020—lasted 15 weeks) and soon to overtake the second wave (January 2021-lasted nearly 9 weeks)
- The third wave could last longer than the first two waves
- Additional restriction would be in place for 14 days until evaluation
    - Social gatherings to be halted (political, cultural, social and religious)
    - Attendance for funerals may not exceed more than 50 people
    - Public spaces (beaches and parks) to remain open
    - Curfew from 9 pm—4 am
    - Sale of alcohol prohibited to reduce alcohol-related emergencies in hospitals

Heavenly Hope

- Travel in-and out—of Gauteng province prohibited because of the highest case of infections (with exceptions)
- Limited access to higher education institutions and school closures
- All health protocols to be maintained by businesses (mandatory to wear a face mask; reduce physical attendance at workplaces)
- National vaccination roll-out plant to continue according to priority groups e.g. healthcare workers, pensioners (Johnson & Johnson; Pfizer)

In this case, South Africa quickly had to adjust to a new mode of thinking, since some of these changes had to be implemented just hours after the report had been given. Most businesses, restaurants, churches and workplaces had to execute these changes immediately to stay out of the trouble of being prosecuted. This really put a huge strain on the usual operations of almost every work environment as most people battled to submit to the authorities and adapt to this 'new normal' way of doing business.

How could we possibly survive these ever-changing conditions?

In a prayer that Jesus made for his disciples in John 17 right before his crucifixion, he asked God to grant them safety in this world because he knew that they would face a lot of discomfort and dangers of death during rough seasons. As God's children, we understand that we have special favor in the Lord's eyes, meaning that we have extra protection from these kinds of plagues that may catch us off guard. Jesus stated, *"I'm not asking you to take them out of the world, but to keep them safe from the evil one. They do not belong to this world any more than I do."* (John 17:15-16). In this passage, Jesus knew full well that there would be danger ahead for his disciples for preaching the Gospel and that they would fall into the temptation of giving up when things got tough or cast away their faith when the worries of life got in the way. But we are reminded in this third memory verse that we not of this world, but citizens of heaven, meaning that we have greater advantage over most, if not *all* the things this world could possibly throw at us—*"And my righteous ones will live by faith. But I will take no pleasure in anyone who turns away."* (Heb 10:38).

". . . where the Lord Jesus Christ lives . . . "
(Phil 3:20)

The Apostle John reminds us not to fall into despair in times of crisis, and not to get so consumed and worked up by the things of this realm that we presently find ourselves in, but to rather focus on the gift of eternal life that we inherited when we first believed in God's Son, Jesus Christ. In his letter to the church in Philippi, he makes clear the importance of this salvation we have, that it is simply based on pure and genuine love for God, and not for this world or the things that it offers—*"this world is fading away, along with everything that people crave. But anyone who does what pleases God will live forever."* (1 John 2:17).

The gospel of Luke also gives an accurate record of this salvation we have in Jesus, that as saints living in this dark world, God has given us many gifts to perform certain things that we've have been called out to do as disciples that can further attest to our faith in salvation—to heal the sick, to cast out demons and basically, to demonstrate the inherent power we possess by the Holy Spirit. And although these gifts are all good and well, and serve a fantastic purpose for displaying God's glory, Jesus points out that this is not a reason enough to be happy-*"But don't rejoice because evil spirits obey you; rejoice because your names are registered in heaven."* (Luke 10:20).

Paul further reiterates this by stating in his letter to the church in Colossae saying *"Since you have been raised to new life with Christ, set your sights on the realities of heaven, where Christ sits in the place of honor at God's right hand. Think about the things of heaven, not the things of earth. For you died to this life, and your real life is hidden with Christ in God."*(Col 3:1–3). But can our minds make real sense of this? How can we just become immune to the effects of the pandemic around us when we have not made our way to heaven yet? How can we simply overlook what's going on around us and not afraid or concerned for the world, for our own souls, and the consequences that this pandemic could have on those around us? What does it really mean to be a citizen of heaven while we are still here on earth? And how can we fix our eyes on the realities of heaven which most of us haven't even had the awesome privilege to see?

In the book of Colossians, Paul starts out by first commending the church for their faith in Christ, their love for God's people, which come from their confident hope of what God has reserved for them in heaven (Col 1:3). Clearly, this indicates that this church had received some kind of profound revelation of what to expect in the life to come. One of the revelations stated in this book is that Christ lives in us, and we will therefore share in his glory (Col 1:27). Jesus also reminded his disciples of this—"*When everything is ready, I will come and get you, so that you will always be with me where I am. And you know the way to where I am going.*" (John 14:3).

In the meanwhile, Paul encouraged the Colossians not to drift away from this promise that Jesus Christ gave, not to get caught up in civilian affairs and further adds that we should refrain from the temptation of falling into confusion—"*Don't let anyone capture you with empty philosophies and high-sounding nonsense that come from human thinking and from the spiritual powers of this world, rather than from Christ.*" (Col 2:8). It is easy for us to get tied up in the affairs of what the politicians and the scientists are saying or predicting about the current pandemic, to lose track of the calling that the Lord has given to us as his children, and to forget that none of what is happening in the world right now is new to God. Paul exhorts the Corinthians who had faced a lot of apostasy in their day because of the distresses and dilemmas saying, "*For we don't look at the troubles we can see now; rather, we fix our gaze on things that cannot be seen. For the things we see now will soon be gone, but the things we cannot see will last forever.*" (2 Cor 4:18). This only means one thing, that what's important for us as Christians is to continually meditate on heaven, *where the Lord Jesus Christ lives*, just as with the people we read about in the Old Testament, where

"... *they were looking for a better place, a heavenly homeland. That is why God is not ashamed to be called their God, for he has prepared a city for them.*" (Heb 11:16).

> "... *And we are eagerly waiting for him to return as our Savior*"
> *(Phil 3:20)*

Our God has given the church spiritual authority to defeat the powers of darkness and to fight for the kingdom of light through prayer and agreement with heaven-"*Now I say to you that you are Peter (which means 'rock'), and upon this rock I will build my church, and all the powers of hell will not conquer it. And I will give you the keys of the Kingdom of Heaven. Whatever you forbid on earth will be forbidden in heaven, and whatever you permit on earth will be permitted in heaven.*" (Matt 16:18-19). This means that the Lord has given the saints the power to change the course of history through the same power that conquered the grave of Jesus, the champion of our faith.

Jesus also revealed an important key to successfully impose godly authority in a world that's become outrageously chaotic. He tells us to, "*Seek the Kingdom of God above all else, and live righteously, and he will give you everything you need.*" (Matt 6:33). 'Everything you need' being everything we need to run the race, finish it and ultimately win the heavenly prize that God has called us to (Phil 3:14). Paul further adds to this by explaining how we can achieve it—"*And now, dear brothers and sisters, one final thing. Fix your thoughts on what is true, and honorable, and right, and pure, and lovely, and admirable. Think about things that are excellent and worthy of praise.*" (Phil 4:8). What does that mean for us in this current pandemic or any given situation for that matter?

Well, we know that the Bible is full of innumerable keys that lead us to unraveling the kingdom of God. One of greatest importance being to love one another—"*This is my commandment: Love each other in the same way I have loved you*" (John 15:12). Love can be expressed in various forms, including forgiveness of those who have hurt us. "*If you forgive those who sin against you, your heavenly Father will forgive you. But if you refuse to forgive others, your Father will not forgive your sins."* (Matt 6:14). Forgiveness can open many doors in our walk of faith and reveal greater remedies for the current state that the world finds itself in. Not only that, but it reveals the true character of our God and the work of Christ that the Cross of Calvary has accomplished. The letter to Timothy reminds us that, *"If we endure hardship, we will reign with him."* (Tim 2:12), and sometimes forgiving someone may seem like some kind of hardship and almost impossible. We can only depend on God's grace for this.

The Word of God reveals other mysteries about things to look forward to in heaven, and these are our heavenly rewards, otherwise known as crowns—*"I am coming soon. Hold on to what you have, so that no one will take away your crown."* (Rev 3:11). God designed crowns to express honor, glory and beauty, probably one of our most prized possessions we'll ever inherit forever. The Bible also speaks of these different rewards for different tasks that we perform well while we are still here on earth. For this reason, Paul tells Timothy that, *"Physical training is good, but training for godliness is much better, promising benefits in this life and in the life to come."* (1 Tim 4:8). Meaning that there's still yet more to come when we get to heaven, rewards that we can start working towards while God's grace still allows us to, and these will be given out at the judgment seat of Christ, otherwise known as the Bema seat of God—*"So whether we are here in this body or away from this body, our goal is to please him. For we must all stand before Christ to be judged. We will each receive whatever we deserve for the good or evil we have done in this earthly body."* (2 Cor 5:9–10).

CROWNS
ETERNAL REWARDS FROM HEAVEN

Crown of LIFE
(For suffering for his name's sake)
James 1:12 & Revelation 2:10

Crown of GLORY
(For those who feed the flock)
1 Peter 5:4

Crown of REJOICING
(For those who win souls)
1 Thessalonians 2:19

Crown of RIGHTEOUSNESS
(For those looking forward to his appearing)
2 Timothy 4:8

INCORRUPTIBLE Crown
(For those who faithfully run the race to win)
1 Corinthians 9:25

THE CROWN OF LIFE (FOR SUFFERING FOR HIS NAME'S SAKE)

> *"God blesses those who patiently endure testing and temptation. Afterward they will receive the crown of life that God has promised to those who love him."*
> ***(Jas 1:12)***

This crown is received by overcoming temptations that we face in our daily walk of faith with Christ Jesus and making use of God-given strategies to walk in victory when we are being tempted to do evil or to sin. To receive this crown, we are meant to reject the idea of focusing on the wrong things so that we can win over the evil one who tempts us, and that is Satan. Temptation is a time when you are given the choice between life and death in a situation as is stated in the Old Testament when Moses laid out all the points and sub-points about what it meant for God's people to be holy like God in all their ways saying, *"Today I have given you the choice between life and death, between blessings and curses. Now I call on heaven and earth to witness the choice you make. Oh, that you would choose life, so that you and your descendants might live!"* (Deut 30:19).

James further makes it clear that God is not responsible for our temptations—*"And remember, when you are being tempted, do not say, "God is tempting me." God is never tempted to do wrong, and he never tempts anyone else."* (Jas 1:13). James also brings a reminder of the words of Jesus where he told his disciples that, *"If you love me, obey my commandments."* (John 14:15). And so this crown in a sense, is not only for the temporary victories that we experience on earth, which are not even worth boasting about, but it's an eternal crown that is given for somebody who has been approved on the day of judgment, someone who the Lord validates as one who really showed themselves worthy of living up to fighting the temptations for the sake of Christ.

The second verse relating to the crown of life is found in Rev 2:10, where the Lord Jesus Christ gives a letter to the church in Smyrna—*"Don't be afraid of what you are about to suffer. The devil will throw some of you into prison to test you. You will suffer for ten days. But if you remain faithful even when facing death, I will give you the crown of life."* (Rev 2:10). The Christians in Smyrna would be trialed and tested, and they'd be expected to pass the test to receive this reward. This church, together with the church in Philadelphia, had no complaint spoken against it, compared to the other five. It has survived through centuries of Roman and Muslim persecution, and could therefore be taken as a picture of the church of today that holds on to their faith in Christ amidst all the persecution, and possibly the saints that would reject the worship of the antichrist during the Great Tribulation.

> *"The Christians in Smyrna suffered under persecution, and they were afraid. Sometimes we think that Christians who endure persecution are almost super-human, and we sometimes don't appreciate the depths of fear they struggle with. There were things which they were about to*

suffer, and Jesus wanted them ready to stand against those things."[2]

THE CROWN OF GLORY (FOR THOSE WHO FEED THE FLOCK)

> "And when the Great Shepherd appears, you will receive a crown of never-ending glory and honor." (1 Pet 5:4)

One of the most loving things you can do for Jesus is to love his sheep like a true shepherd would—*"Your love for one another will prove to the world that you are my disciples."* (John 13:35). Peter, who had denied Jesus three times before he was crucified, met again with Jesus after his resurrection. This happened the third time he appeared to his disciples beside the Sea of Galilee on the beach, and it gave Peter a wonderful opportunity to recommit to the Lord after having messed up so many times before:

> "After breakfast Jesus asked Simon Peter,
> "Simon son of John, do you love me more than these?"
> "Yes, Lord," Peter replied, "you know I love you."
> "Then feed my lambs," Jesus told him.
> Jesus repeated the question:
> "Simon son of John, do you love me?"
> "Yes, Lord," Peter said, "you know I love you."
> "Then take care of my sheep," Jesus said.
> A third time he asked him,
> "Simon son of John, do you love me?"
> Peter was hurt that Jesus asked the question a third time.
> He said, "Lord, you know everything. You know that I love you."
> Jesus said, "Then feed my sheep."
> *(John 21:15-17)*

---

2. Guzik, "Revelation 2."

HEAVENLY HOPE

In this brief dialog, Jesus gives Peter a challenge to grow and to stretch his faith by looking after the church, and that is the flock of the Lord's sheepfold, both the sheep and the lambs alike. Previously, Jesus had declared Peter's position as the 'rock' or the foundation of the church, telling him that he'd been given the keys to the kingdom. We see throughout the gospels that Jesus kept training Peter while he was still on earth with him, teaching him how to master the art of faith. It seems Peter had done just that, when he saw his Master again on the beach in this instance, and having no sense of guilt or shame for having denied him, but rather much joy to see him again. And this is where Jesus could entrust him to feed his disciples, similarly to how Elijah handed down his responsibility to his protégé, Elisha.

In this case, we understand that the life of faith comes with having to develop maturity. As we grow in our walk of faith with the Lord, we are entrusted with more responsibilities— *"When someone has been given much, much will be required in return; and when someone has been entrusted with much, even more will be required."* (Luke 12:48). Peter, who'd received much nurturing, shepherding and training from the Lord himself, was no exception, and this includes the church and all mature believers in the faith. The Lord expected Peter to pass down what he had learnt. No wonder this great revelation was given to him to in 1 Pet 5:4, that there would be a reward for this at the end of it all, an eternal crown of glory for looking after God's people— *"Now these are the gifts Christ gave to the church: the apostles, the prophets, the evangelists, and the pastors and teachers. Their responsibility is to equip God's people to do his work and build up the church, the body of Christ."* (Eph 4:11-12).

The Apostle Paul makes this clear that, *"Because of God's grace to me, I have laid the foundation like an expert builder. Now others are building on it. But whoever is building on this foundation must be very careful. For no one can lay any foundation other than the one we already have—Jesus Christ. Anyone who builds on that foundation may use a variety of materials—gold, silver, jewels, wood, hay, or straw. But on the judgment day, fire will reveal what kind of work each builder has done. The fire will show if a person's work has any value. If the work survives, that builder will receive a reward."* (1 Cor 3:10–14). And so, it is not only about serving in the church that'll win the shepherds the prize, but the quality of work that is produced.

THE CROWN OF REJOICING (FOR THOSE WHO WIN SOULS)

> *"After all, what gives us hope and joy, and what will be our proud reward and crown as we stand before our Lord Jesus when he returns? It is you!"* (1 Thess 2:19)

This crown is designated for soul winners, evangelists, people that devote their time to spreading the Gospel to the public by either preaching or through personal witness which leads sinners to repentance and salvation. This could be thought of as an 'alter call', a traditional call at the end of a church service that serves to invite people to come forward publicly and make a new spiritual commitment with this verse in mind—*"If you openly declare that Jesus is Lord and believe in your heart that God raised him from the dead, you will be saved."* (Rom 10:9). Repentance before the Lord and the church or other witnesses is then made, following this typical example of Billy Graham's sinner's prayer that is based on the "ABC" principle: A-Admitting that you're a sinner; B-Believing that Jesus died for your sins and rose again; C-Confessing that Jesus is the Lord:

> *"Dear Lord Jesus, I know that I am a sinner, and I ask for Your forgiveness.*
> *I believe You died for my sins and rose from the dead.*
> *I turn from my sins and invite You to come into my heart and life.*
> *I want to trust and follow You as my Lord and Savior.*
> *In Your Name.*
> *Amen."*

Luke 15 gives three different parables where Jesus describes the joy of finding the lost. First, he compares it to a lost sheep—*"In the same way, there is more joy in heaven over one lost sinner who repents and returns to God than over ninety-nine others who are righteous and haven't strayed away!"* (Luke 15:7); a lost coin—*"And when she finds it, she will call in her friends and neighbors and say, 'Rejoice with me because I have found my lost coin.'"* (Luke 15:9); and a lost son—*"We had to celebrate this happy day. For your brother was dead and has come back to life! He was lost, but now he is found!"* (Luke 15:32). Clearly these statements point out the rejoicing that takes place in heaven when even one sinner repents and commits their life to the Lord. This pleases God, and there is certainly an eternal reward for this, the crown of glory for the workers who harvest these souls.

James further states that, *"You can be sure that whoever brings the sinner back from wandering will save that person from death and bring about the forgiveness of many sins."* (Jas 5:20), meaning that there is an eternal reward for one who saves somebody from sins that could've otherwise led them to hell and eternal damnation—*"In the same way, there is joy in the presence of God's angels when even one sinner repents."* (Luke 15:10). One of the reasons this comes with a reward is because it's no easy job. Soul winners are meant to walk the walk, and talk the talk to convince or lead an unbeliever to Christ. This requires the righteousness that comes from *Jehovah Tsidkenu* that enables the lost to be saved by clearly explaining the scriptures, as with the story of Philip and the Ethiopian Eunuch (Acts 8: 26–40). Peter adds that, *"if someone asks about your hope as a believer, always be ready to explain it."* (1 Pet 3:15).

THE CROWN OF RIGHTEOUSNESS (FOR THOSE LOOKING FORWARD TO HIS APPEARING)

> *"And now the prize awaits me—the crown of righteousness, which the Lord, the righteous Judge, will give me on*

the day of his return. And the prize is not just for me but for all who eagerly look forward to his appearing." (2 Tim 4:8)

This crown was Paul's final testimony to Timothy as he sat in his cold prison cell with the understanding that even under those dire conditions, there was a spiritual reality the extended beyond his imprisonment. After having being in the ministry for 30 years, Paul still believed in the second coming of Christ with all of his heart, and was earnestly awaiting his appearance that would've saved him from his torment of isolation. Paul's earliest letters such as 1 and 2 Thess testify about the rapture when he says, *"For the Lord himself will come down from heaven with a commanding shout, with the voice of the archangel, and with the trumpet call of God. First, the believers who have died will rise from their graves. Then, together with them, we who are still alive and remain on the earth will be caught up in the clouds to meet the Lord in the air. Then we will be with the Lord forever."* (1 Thess 4:16–17). In his indication, he exhorted Timothy to never give up on preaching the Word, and to never be ashamed of the testimony of Jesus, adding that he should, *"Hold on to the pattern of wholesome teaching you learned from me—a pattern shaped by the faith and love that you have in Christ Jesus."* (2 Tim 1:13).

He further encouraged Timothy to be vigilant and to be ready to take on all kinds of afflictions that would come with preaching the Gospel, which is no surprise since Jesus warned his disciples of the same persecutions. The point of Paul's warnings were basically to prepare Timothy's heart for taking on a fully surrendered life to the ministry. This meant having to deny the world and take up the cross daily, to live a completely surrendered life and to be 100% committed to doing the work of an evangelist in fulfilling the ministry of Christ. Most of our pastors live this kind of life. And thankfully, Paul had an eternal prize in mind for this. This was also testified by the Apostle John who said, *"Dear friends, we are already God's children, but he has not yet shown us what we will be like when Christ appears. But we do know that we will be like him, for we will see him as he really is. And all who have this eager expectation will keep themselves pure, just as he is pure."* (1 John 3:2-4).

Paul's triumphant confidence came from this promise that he'd been fully convinced about. He was at the end of his life knowing that just like everybody else, he was going to depart this earth eventually. He knew that he had fought the good fight of faith, he'd done all that he could do to get himself approved by Christ, and he was confident that that he'd done a good job. This is amazing. And this gives us the same confidence as we continue our walk of faith with the Lord and that one day Jesus will be happy with us—*"The master was full of praise. 'Well done, my good and faithful servant. You have been faithful in handling this small amount, so now I will give you many more responsibilities. Let's celebrate together!"* (Matt 25:23).

In the first epistle of John, we are warned not to love this world, not to get attached or settle down, since this is only our temporary residence anyway. John says, *"Do not love this world nor the things it offers you, for when you love the world, you do not have the love of the Father in you.* (1 John 2:15). If the church keeps this in mind, and we focus our attention to this truth, looking forward to Christ's appearing, we are sure not to miss out on this heavenly crown-*"Now you have every spiritual gift you need as you eagerly wait for the return of our Lord Jesus Christ. He will keep you strong to the end so that you will be free from all blame on the day when our Lord Jesus Christ returns."* (1 Cor 1:7-8).

THE INCORRUPTIBLE CROWN (FOR THOSE WHO FAITHFULLY RUN THE RACE TO WIN)

> *"All athletes are disciplined in their training. They do it to win a prize that will fade away, but we do it for an eternal prize."* (1 Cor 9:25)

Here, the Apostle Paul compares the saints to athletes who are meant to train diligently to build up their physical strength and endurance. Athletes have to be disciplined, or else they will lose the race and miss out on the prize. Comprehensive training allows athletes improve the cognitive skills, build motivation and ambition for the trophy or medal that's ahead, and so it is necessary that they stick to an athlete's diet of some sort and do the necessary amount of training to build up their power and strength. The same goes with all Christians. We have spiritual disciplines that we need to stick to on a daily or regular basis, and these may include activities that inspire us to fulfill the ministry of Christ that God has called us to without wavering or getting beat down. Having daily devotions is one of them, as well as a committed prayer life, or attending church services. All these and more strengthen the life of a Christian and keeps us focused. There is a heavenly prize for being disciplined and not allowing the things of this world distract us or get us off course. This is the incorruptible crown.

"Men of Galilee," they said, *"why are you standing here staring into heaven? Jesus has been taken from you into heaven, but someday he will return from heaven in the same way you saw him go!"* (Acts 1:11). In this verse, Luke records the events that took place before the inception of the church, the day of Pentecost. This happened when two white-robed men appeared to the apostles who had just seen Jesus after his crucifixion —*"Once when he was eating with them, he commanded them, "Do not leave Jerusalem until the Father sends you the gift he promised, as I told you before. John baptized with water, but in just a few days you will be baptized with the Holy Spirit."* (Acts 1:4–5). This happened ten days later. His disciples didn't know when he would come back, and so they kept pressing him for an answer. He simply replied, *"The Father alone has the authority to set those dates and times, and they are not for you to know"* (Acts 1:7). He gave them his last instruction, that while they wait for his return, they should go and witness to people all over the world about him. And after that, he was taken up into heaven.

These two white-robed men were sent as messengers to tell the apostles that it's time to get to work. Staring into the sky and wondering when Jesus would come back was not part of this work. Jesus had given them a clear instruction of the work ahead—*"But you will receive power when the Holy Spirit comes upon you. And you will be my witnesses, telling people about me everywhere—in Jerusalem, throughout Judea, in Samaria, and to the ends of the earth."* (Acts 1:8). This the work of witnessing goes beyond self-isolation. It means that as disciples of Jesus, we are meant to go out there to the people that God has placed around us, whether physically or virtually (since some are still on lockdown during this pandemic) and to give a witness about Jesus, to testify about him and to extend the same grace of salvation we received. For this kind of work, discipline is required. But thankfully, by the power of the Holy Spirit we have received this spirit—*"For God has not given us a spirit of fear and timidity, but of power, love, and self-discipline."* (2 Tim 1:7). And self-discipline will keep us fit to do the work of the ministry.

> "And remember that the heavenly Father to whom you pray has no favorites. He will judge or reward you according to what you do. So you must live in reverent fear of him during your time here as "temporary residents."
>
> (1 PET 1:17)

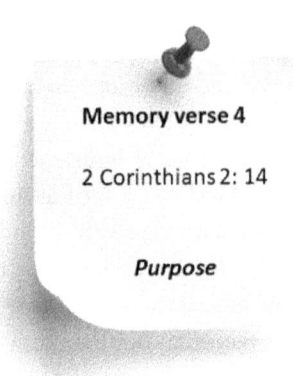

"But thank God! He has made us his captives and continues to lead us along in Christ's triumphal procession. Now he uses us to spread the knowledge of Christ everywhere, like a sweet perfume"

-2 Corinthians 2: 14

Chapter 4
PURPOSE

JEHOVAH RAAH IS THE Hebrew name for God meaning "The Lord my Shepherd" taken straight from a very famous beloved poem of David found in Ps 23, *"The Lord is my shepherd; I have all that I need . . . "* Henry Ward Beecher, an American clergyman known for his support of the abolition of slavery once described Psalm 23 in these prolific words:

"*It has charmed more griefs to rest than all the philosophy of the world. It has remanded to their dungeon more felon thoughts, more black doubts, more thieving sorrows, than there are sands on the seashore. It has comforted the noble host of the poor. It has sung courage*

Purpose

to the army of the disappointed. It has poured balm and consolation into the heart of the sick, of captives in dungeons, of widows in their pinching griefs, of orphans in their loneliness. Dying soldiers have died easier as it was read to them; ghastly hospitals have been illuminated; it has visited the prisoner, and broken his chains, and, like Peter's angel, led him forth in imagination, and sung him back to his home again. It has made the dying Christian slave freer than his master, and consoled those whom, dying, he left behind mourning, not so much that he was gone, as because they were left behind, and could not go, too."[1]

The Bible commentator, James Montgomery Boice also added the following:

"Millions of people have memorized this psalm, even those who have learned few other Scripture portions. Ministers have used it to comfort people who are going through severe personal trials, suffering illness, or dying. For some, the words of this psalm have been the last they have ever uttered in life."[2]

King David is one of the Bible's most compelling characters, famously known to be a giant slayer, conqueror, and a young shepherd who ascended to the throne of Israel to be the king of God's people, and is presumed to later be the prince of Israel during the millennial age to come (Ezek 37:24–25). David, much like Jesus was born in Bethlehem in the land of Judah (907 BC), being the youngest of seven sons of Jesse and a descendant of Ruth, the Moabite convert (Matt 1:5). Before becoming king, David had served the first king of Israel, Saul as a skilled musician who played the harp to ease his predecessor's tormented soul after he'd sinned against God by giving a sacrifice that only the priest was allowed to give (1 Sam 13).

Later, David was persistently challenged by a bitter king Saul, who wanted him dead after having realized that David would be his successor. David also had to go through the agony of facing the Philistine giant, Goliath who kept appearing to the Israelites for 40 days taunting them to fight against him-*"Why are you all coming out to fight?"* he called. *"I am the Philistine champion, but*

---

1. Spurgeon, *"Spurgeon's Treasury of David"*
2. James Montgomery Boice, quoted in Guzik, *"Psalm 23."*

you are only the servants of Saul. Choose one man to come down here and fight me! If he kills me, then we will be your slaves. But if I kill him, you will be our slaves!" (1 Sam 17:8–9). When the young David managed to take Goliath down with only a shepherd staff, a slingshot and five stones, this marked him as a national hero granting him fame and power that would one day help him usurp the throne.

In the prime of his life, at the age of 30, David was wise in counsel, prompt in action and God-fearing, making the people recognize him as the most suitable candidate for the throne, much like Jesus who started his ministry at the same age. David had many wives and concubines, however the Bible only mentions about eight, including Bathsheba, Uriah's wife, who David married after having conspired the death of her husband in battle. David was later confronted by the Prophet Nathan about this sin. He ended up pronouncing judgment against David, which would be the death of their first infant son (2 Sam 12:4).

Having read this story, it seems clear why King David could have been involved in so much trouble and agony, as we reflect on his songs and poems in the book of Psalm. He was very much human and quite crafty in his dealings. Nonetheless, the most important lesson we can take from David's life, apart from his excellent natural skills and wits is that he always found favor with God. The Lord chose a person like David because he proved to be a man after God's own heart despite all his flaws. He continually demonstrated his faith by staying committed to Yahweh and because of this, God recognized him to be a good shepherd for the nation of Israel.

> *"But thank God! He has made us his captives and continues to lead us along in Christ's triumphal procession . . . "*
> *(2 Cor 2:14)*

From David's life, it's easy to question his authenticity as *really* a 'man after God's own heart'? It's also easy to forget to look back at our own lives, and see how much grace the Lord has had on us for our past and present sins, and the mistakes we continually make.

It's easy to hold a grudge against a neighbor who's wronged us and we sometimes refuse to let it go. Why? Perhaps because, we might feel more superior than they are? That the grace we've received from God was earned by our so-called merits? In fact it's almost like condemning David in this instance, the man whose songs and poems we all ever-so often love to quote, and yet at times our hearts still condemn him for what he did with Bathsheba, which is exactly what we do when we refuse to forgive somebody who has wronged us.

Well then I guess we can always take courage in this fourth memory verse, really reflect on God's mercy upon our own personal lives too, and to simply just thank him! Thank him that he took our emptiness, brokenness, weaknesses and our many, many sins away. And thank him that he saved us and took us captive by nailing our old lives on the cross with him, graciously giving us a new life and a heavenly purpose—*"For God saved us and called us to live a holy life. He did this, not because we deserved it, but because that was his plan from before the beginning of time—to show us his grace through Christ Jesus."* (2 Tim 1:9).

For this reason, David never backed down even after sinning because, *"The godly may trip seven times, but they will get up again."*(Prov 24:16). David simply confessed his sin to the Lord, repented and carried on with the race. He is called 'a man after God's own heart' because his purpose was engraved deep into his heart, and this was to seek the Lord and serve the Him faithfully, without allowing anything to take that purpose away. As children of God, we are to take on the same mindset, to realize that we are not at all perfect, we all make mistakes, but this should never get in the way of our heavenly purpose, or keep us down when we have fallen or backslidden. We are to take on Paul's attitude when he said, *"I press on to reach the end of the race and receive the heavenly prize for which God, through Christ Jesus, is calling us."* (Phil 3:14).

Many people still carry this idea that the COVID-19 pandemic is the first of its kind, a pandemic that the world has never witnessed before, and may possibly even point to the total eradication of all humanity. This leaves us with very little hope for living out the life that Christ has set for us. But we know that there *have* been other global pandemics before and this may not be the end of it all.

The Justinianic plague around 541–549 AD was the first major outbreak, the first Old World pandemic caused by bacterium known as *Yersinia pestis*, a serious microbe that's responsible for three of the deadliest pandemics recorded in history (including the Black Death which followed after that). This contagious disease was carried from Egypt and affected the entire Mediterranean Basin, Europe and the Near East, through a recently conquered Egypt paying tribute to Emperor Justinian in grain. Supposedly, this plague was carried by fleas that hitched a ride on the black rats that snacked on the grain. This led to its decimation in Constatinople, ultimately spreading like wildfire across Europe, Asia, North Africa and Arabia and killing an estimated 30 to 50 million people, about half of the world's population.[3]

People merely survived through the plague without any *real* medical intervention, except for avoiding the sick at the time. However, about 800 years later between 1347 and 1351, the plague returned again, this time killing with reckless abandon. This bubonic plague, known as the most fatal pandemic recorded in human history claimed about 200 million lives in just four years.[4] At the time, forced isolation for 40 days or 'quarantino', was the only best way to stop the spread of the disease. It seems that London never really got a chance to rest after the Black Death.

The plague managed to somehow resurface roughly every 10 years from 1348 to 1665, about 40 outbreaks in just over 300 years. By the early 1500s, England imposed the first laws to separate and isolate the sick, quite similar to 'social distancing' imposed by our governments. However, in those days, this seemed much more publicly intensified because homes that were stricken by the plague had to be marked with a bale of hay strung on a pole outside, and people with infected family members residing in that home were expected to carry a white pole whenever they went out in public. And much like what's seen today with this coronavirus outbreak,

3. Than, "Two of History's deadliest plagues"
4. Shipman, "*The bright side of the black death*", 410

all public entertainment was banned, forcing victims 'stay at home' to prevent the spread of the disease, in addition to red crosses being painted on their doors along with a plea of forgiveness, "Lord have mercy on us".

Today, as we continue to make the confession to those around us that we *are* indeed saved and that we belong to the Lord, made to be his captives through the his mercy, we should take note of the words in this fourth memory verse, where Paul starts off by expressing his gratitude for this. Here, Paul writes these words straight after he suggested that the church in Corinth should forgive the brother who had sinned amongst them. And although the Bible does not mention who this man is, some Bible scholars suppose that it could've been the same man that Paul had urged the church to confront about living immorally with his stepmother, and to handle the matter by throwing him out to Satan until he repented (1 Cor 5).

Paul was well aware of the devil's strategies. He urged the church to take precaution in these matters of forgiving this man's sin and to receive him back into the church. Paul further continued to minister to them about the New Covenant of grace by first dealing with the probable criticism that he would get from the church about his capricious travel plans that delayed his message. He explained to them that he'd not been ready to preach the Gospel of Christ because he hadn't yet received a report from Titus about them, and so he set off to go find him first (2 Cor 2:12–13). Although it may have sounded like an excuse for his clumsiness, Paul needed to make it clear to the church that his ultimate plan was to follow Christ and preach the Gospel in all its fullness. This could only be done by having to overcome every hurdle that would hinder the effectiveness of his preaching.

We see that as Paul gets into his message about the New Covenant, he acknowledges the grace of God's salvation and the overwhelming power of Christ that led to his captivity and servitude. The Bible scholar William Barclay compares Paul's experience to a Roman triumph, a spectacular celebration parade held in the ancient city of Rome for a military commander who had won an important victory on the battlefield:

> "*In a Triumph the procession of the victorious general marched through the streets of Rome to the Capitol . . . First came the state officials and the senate. Then came the trumpeters. Then were carried the spoils taken from the conquered land . . . Then came the pictures of the conquered land and models of conquered citadels and ships. There followed the white bull for sacrifice which would be made. Then there walked the captive princes, leaders and generals in chains, shortly to be flung into prison and in all probability almost immediately to be executed. Then came the lictors bearing their rods, followed by the musicians with their lyres; then the priests swinging their censers with the sweet-smelling incense burning in them. After that came the general himself . . . finally came the army wearing all their decorations and shouting Io triumphe! Their cry of triumph. As the procession moved through the streets, all decorated and garlanded, amid the cheering crowds, it made a tremendous day which might happen only once in a lifetime.*" [5]

". . . Now he uses us to spread the knowledge of Christ everywhere, like a sweet perfume" (2 Cor 2:14)

The ministry of Jesus on earth including all his miracles and teachings follow the description of what true worship is in the words of the Prophet Isaiah—"*Share your food with the hungry, and give shelter to the homeless. Give clothes to those who need them, and do not hide from relatives who need your help.* "*Then your salvation will come like the dawn, and your wounds will quickly heal. Your godliness will lead you forward, and the glory of the Lord will protect you from behind.*" (Isa 58:7–8). From this we see that in the New Testament, the church was given the same ministry. Jesus explained in the Gospel of John that he is the Good Shepherd, *Jehovah Raah*, who tends after his flock and makes sure that not a single one of his followers is devoured by the enemy. This very same protection is made available to us, the church as we follow in Christ's footsteps and tend after the flock that he has given to us,

5. Barclay's Daily Bible Study

being it our relatives, neighbors, friends, colleagues, strangers, the homeless, orphans or foreigners.

The purpose of our existence as believers is outlined in the Great Commission given by Jesus—*"Therefore, go and make disciples of all the nations, baptizing them in the name of the Father and the Son and the Holy Spirit. Teach these new disciples to obey all the commands I have given you. And be sure of this: I am with you always, even to the end of the age."* (Matt 28:19–20). In this last passage of Matthew's Gospel, the Lord ends his command with a promise that he would be with his disciples throughout their ministry until the end of their lives. *Jehovah Raah*, the Good Shepherd would guard and protect them as they lived out their duties on earth, and his promise still stands for us today.

Throughout his ministry, Jesus often included some guidelines and eternal benefits that came with faithfully carrying out these assignments. These add tremendous value to the purpose of our ministry as believers and reasons for staying alive. Jesus taught his disciples and gave them keys to a successful ministry in the form of beatitudes and parables, basically creative ways that led to their understanding of God's character and genuine faith that expresses the faithfulness of Yahweh—*"for I will speak to you in a parable. I will teach you hidden lessons from our past."* (Ps 78:2). These followers must haves surely felt motivated by the idea that they would be rewarded in heaven for their work on earth, amidst all the persecution that was ahead of their ministry (Luke 6:17–23).

Jesus also added that putting in hard work in making disciples produces wonderful results—*"When you produce much fruit, you are my true disciples. This brings great glory to my Father."* (John 15:8). The Apostle Paul exhorted the church in Philippi to adapt to this way of thinking, and share the same goal as believers in the faith. It's a mutual partnership and shows our faithfulness towards him—*"Then make me truly happy by agreeing wholeheartedly with each other, loving one another, and working together with one mind and purpose."* (Phil 2:2). In this way, we converge our minds together to the calling of serving Christ, we devotedly stick to it and we choose not to allow the worries of this life blind our shared hope, or this pandemic to cloud the purpose we have of spreading the knowledge of Christ 'like a sweet perfume'—"*Let your conversation be gracious and attractive so that you will have the right response for everyone.*" (Col 4:6). We do this by seasoning our words with salt, and adding flavor to the message we give to those around us. And sometimes this takes the creative work of the Holy Spirit or a spark that ignites us to add a glimmer of hope to a hurting soul that needs Jesus.

We do this by taking courage in *Jehovah Raah* -"*For God has said, "I will never fail you. I will never abandon you."* (Heb 13:5). The Lord is not only our king and shepherd, but he is also our bridegroom, our inheritance of whom we love, our Lord that we're eagerly waiting for. Often times, we forget that the Jesus truly does love us, his church, his bride, and that we too are *his* inheritance, as Paul pointed out, "*I pray that your hearts will be flooded with light so that you can understand the confident hope he has given to those he called—his holy people who are his rich and glorious inheritance.*" (Eph 1:18). And so it goes both ways. He's our inheritance (Ps 16:5), in as much as we are his. And it gives the Lord great pleasure to prepare his bride for himself. He did this by showing his obedience to cross and sending us his Spirit to comfort us while we wait for his return—" . . . *overwhelming victory is ours through Christ, who loved us.*" (Heb 8:37).

This law of love that God has called us to is one of the most important virtues that prepares us to meet him. Jesus first commands us to love him with all that we are, our soul, mind and strength, and then also adds the second commandment, with the same value as the first, that we are to love our neighbor as we love ourselves (Matt 22:37–40). Paul emphasizes on this and says, "*Owe nothing to anyone—except for your obligation to love one another. If you love your neighbor, you will fulfill the requirements of God's law.*" (Rom 8:13). Without love, doing anything in faith is almost useless. And although faith pleases God, it adds only little value, if any, to do the work the Lord has called us to.

For it was love that motivated the Good Samaritan to stop everything he was doing to help the traveller who who'd been stripped off his clothes, beaten and left half dead on the road (Luke 10:25-37). It was through love that Joseph of Arimathea took the time to go and bury the body of Jesus after his crucifixion (Matt 27:57-61). And it was indeed through the power of love that Jesus decided to go over to Martha and Mary's home to raise Lazarus from the dead (John 11:1-44). All these charitable acts where done in the name of love, not faith alone.

The bride of Christ, being the church, needs to master the art of love as we fulfill the Lord's purpose of the ministry given to us. During Christ's ministry, he made an important note about the work that had been laid out for his followers, those who claimed to believe in him and love him-*"He said to his disciples, "The harvest is great, but the workers are few."* (Matt 9:37). Jesus realized that not many in the world found it easy to carry out this ministry of spreading the Good News because that meant having to do it in love and forgiveness, which is not always easy when the world hates you—*"If you love only those who love you, what reward is there for that? Even corrupt tax collectors do that much. If you are kind only to your friends, how are you different from anyone else? Even pagans do that. But you are to be perfect, even as your Father in heaven is perfect."* (Matt 5:46-48). Jesus later revealed to the Apostle John that he would reward those who are his, who follow his commandments and those who would endure to the end—*"Look, I am coming soon, bringing my reward with me to repay all people according to their deeds."* (Rev 22:12). And so although faith is very much important in our Christian walk, the greatest remains to be love to effectively spread the knowledge of Christ. Paul has more to say about love in 1 Cor 13.

> *"Let us be glad and rejoice,*
> *and let us give honor to him.*
> *For the time has come for the wedding feast of the Lamb,*
> *and his bride has prepared herself."*
>
> (Rev 19:7)

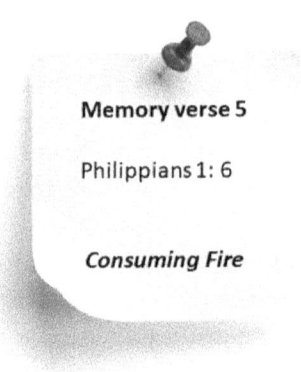

Memory verse 5

Philippians 1: 6

Consuming Fire

"And I am certain that God, who began the good work within you, will continue his work until it is finally finished on the day when Christ Jesus returns."

-Philippians 1: 6

Chapter 5
Consuming Fire

JEHOVAH M'KADDESH MEANING "THE Lord Who Sanctifies You" is the Hebrew name for God taken from Lev 20. The word 'sanctify' means to consecrate or to set apart, to make clean, to purify and to make holy. It's a process for every believer who has surrendered their life to Christ that takes place from the beginning of salvation and justification by the blood of Jesus, and ends with glorification, when we ultimately make it to heaven to live with him. This makes sanctification a central part of our daily life as Christians. There's just no other way but to be made holy, and only God is able to do this. Genesis 2:3 explains the word *'kaddesh'* taken from *Jehovah*

M'kaddesh as holy, where in the process of creation, the Lord set apart the seventh day as the Sabbath and made it a day of rest and completion. We're all in the process of being purified as we live out our Christian walk of faith. Meaning that when we fail or fall short of God's glorious standards by the sins and the struggles we encounter, the myriad of temptations we fall into or the fears that leave us hopeless, we are reminded that the Lord is faithful in who He says He is. He remains the same forever, and He is able to cleanse us of all iniquity and make us who He created us to be– *"For the Scriptures say, "You must be holy because I am holy."* (1 Pet 1:16).

In the book of Leviticus, many sacrifices were made by the priests on behalf of God's people as offerings to the Lord for various reasons, one of them being the atonement of sin according to the laws of Moses. A sacrifice usually involved taking on the full course of transformation, a renewal of heart and a change of mind to accomplish true repentance. The Bible shows us that under the Old Covenant, God received the smoke of burning sacrifices as a pleasing aroma, as in Lev 1, where the idea of sacrifice was introduced to the Israelites under the Mosaic law given to Moses on Mount Sinai straight after the building of the tabernacle had been completed—*"Then, grasping the bird by its wings, the priest will tear the bird open, but without tearing it apart. Then he will burn it as a burnt offering on the wood burning on the altar. It is a special gift, a pleasing aroma to the Lord."* (Lev 1:17).

The book of Leviticus clearly covers defined procedures and protocols that the priests had to follow to atone not only for their sins, but the sins of the people of Israel, as well as the foreigners that dwelt in their land. For burnt offerings, which signified propitiation for sin and complete surrender, devotion, and commitment to God, a male bull, ram, male goat, male dove, or young pigeon (without blemish) would be counted as a voluntary sacrifice; while all animals without blemish such as a bull, male goat and female goat or lamb, dove or pigeon or a tenth of an ephah of flour -all depending on social class, were mandatory offerings made by those who had sinned unknowingly or were considered unclean in order to attain purification.

In Lev 20, where we first come across *Jehovah M'kaddesh*, the Lord addresses the Israelite community about the penalty of sins, including the idolatry that caused them to worship Molech which led them to sacrificing their children. God was totally against this Canaanite practice, having later revealed to Jeremiah that they had also "... *built pagan shrines to Baal, and there they burn their sons as sacrifices to Baal. I have never commanded such a horrible deed; it never even crossed my mind to command such a thing!*" (Jer 19:5). It seems that this was a perpetual weakness for the Israelites who seemed to have struggled with this sin for many years.

The penalties for sin were stated out clearly for the Israelites who had been convicted for their shameful guilt and had failed to make atonement by making offerings required by the priests that could've otherwise brought them back to their senses before things got out of control. However, Paul reminds us that all these rules and regulations about worship and repentance under the law of Moses were only a prefigure of God's saving grace that would now only require faith in the works of Jesus Christ alone as the ultimate sacrifice—"*These things happened to them as examples for us. They were written down to warn us who live at the end of the age.*" (1 Cor 10:11).

Under the old covenant the Lord had commanded very stringent measures to eradicate the pollution in the land of Israel and further revealed his character that-" ... *I am the Lord who makes you holy.*" (Lev 20:8). This also appeared in Ezekiel's prophecy for the restoration of Israel, where the Lord promised to cleanse the sins of his people by giving them his Holy Spirit—"*Then I will sprinkle clean water on you, and you will be clean. Your filth will be washed away, and you will no longer worship idols. And I will give you a new heart, and I will put a new spirit in you. I will take out your stony, stubborn heart and give you a tender, responsive heart.*" (Ezek 36:25–26).

Today, the Lord still continues to sanctify his people. He rids us of our stubbornness and strongholds that have been set up in our minds usually stemming from our backgrounds, experiences, the media or our immediate environments—our friends, boss or our colleagues who carry with them a different philosophy than the one expressed by Christ. The Lord often rids us of these strongholds through a 'shaking'—an event that happens either on a personal or massive scale in our lives that makes us realize our sin problem. For some it takes years, especially in the case of addictions, where some believers find it hard to break free from their yoke of bondage. But the Apostle Paul reminds us that we are to stay focused to God's Word—*"Don't copy the behavior and customs of this world, but let God transform you into a new person by changing the way you think. Then you will learn to know God's will for you, which is good and pleasing and perfect."* (Rom 12:2). And so it is only through the Lord's intervention that our past precepts and ideologies that contradict God's Word can be exterminated to make us truly pure. Sadly, this does not always happen overnight. It takes time and dedicated prayer to receive optimum deliverance and repentance.

The Apostle Paul also reminds us that, *"God has united you with Christ Jesus. For our benefit God made him to be wisdom itself. Christ made us right with God; he made us pure and holy, and he freed us from sin."* (1 Cor 1:30). This has all been done for us on the cross. All we need to do is step out in faith and take hold of our deliverance-*"For this is how God loved the world: He gave his one and only Son, so that everyone who believes in him will not perish but have eternal life* (John 3:16). All our sins have been laid up on the cross.

But at times, the question remains—to be or not to be? We are faced with countless decisions to make during this present pandemic about whether or not to make a choice about a pressing issue, especially when there's the ongoing inception of new variants that are causing worse disease? How do we deal with having to change our behaviours, our habits and reprogramme our minds to all that we are faced with? Is this God's way of sanctifying us and making us more like Him?

COVID-19 has presented major impediments to its curative intervention simply because the virus causing the disease continues to mutate, and alters its infection antigens much like HIV and other serious viral diseases that have been persistent over the years with no cure. Such a crisis has left millions wondering if they should take the vaccines or not, with serious suspicions that make it even harder to make a conclusive decision. Speculations around the most promising FDA approved vaccine candidates have also created an uproar in different countries about which one is the best suited for the people. The disputes going around the nations almost imitate the contest Elijah had against the priests of Baal about whose God was real—*"Then Elijah stood in front of them and said, "How much longer will you waver, hobbling between two opinions? If the Lord is God, follow him! But if Baal is God, then follow him!"* (1 Kgs 18:21).

Concerns aren't only about which vaccine is best to take, but more about their safety in the first place. Also, some believe that these vaccines could be introducing something that goes beyond what science tells us, some sort of low-key ushering of the antichrist and a new world order that we read about in Rev 13. It then becomes an issue of *having* to allow God to a complete involvement in this process of decision-making and taking the time to reflect on what is *really* going on beneath the surface of our hearts, and what taking the vaccine really means for the individual.

One pandemic where the world witnessed a major breakthrough in science was caused by smallpox, one of history's deadliest diseases having killed more than 300 million people since 1900 alone.[1] The pandemic probably extends beyond what's ever been recorded in human history, since its earliest credible evidence dates back to about 3,000 years ago when smallpox-like rashes were found in in the Egyptian mummies. The global spread of this pandemic has been traced back to the growth of civilization and expanding trade routes over the centuries, having first reported from China and Korea, then spreading to northern Africa, Europe and Western Africa by the 15th century. The African slave trade

1. Flight, "Smallpox"

import further spread it like wildfire to other parts of the world, and by the end of the 18th century, the disease had affected North and South America, the Caribbean and Australia, killing about 3/10 of the people that got it. It was only in 1796 when smallpox could be put to an end by the English physician, Edward Jenner, who used a variolation method to protect people against the disease, what we now know as vaccination.

Since Jenner's treatise in 1801 "on the Origin of the Vaccine inoculation", vaccination became widely accepted leading to the Intensified Eradication Program in 1967 that opened up doors for laboratories in many countries to produce more, higher-quality freeze dried vaccines. It seems this vaccination strategy was able to cure the world from the smallpox pandemic, where the last person in the world to have active smallpox was recorded in late 1975 in Asia, and the last person to die from it in 1978 in England.

By May 1980, the 33rd World Health Assembly had declared the world free of smallpox, almost two centuries since Jenner's vaccine discovery. And so it seems that vaccination strategies have impacted the course of history in saving millions of lives, just as any other medicine, and could perhaps be likened to the curative intents that the Prophet Jeremiah laments about for his people in Judah—"*Is there no medicine in Gilead? Is there no physician there?*" (Jer 8:22).

However, even with the ongoing interventions for COVID-19, there is still a global hesitancy to accept the vaccines. A study conducted during 2020 vaccine trials with a sample of over 13,400 individuals from 19 countries that have been hard-hit by the virus, reported that 72% of participants would likely take the vaccine, 14% would refuse, while 14% would hesitate.[2] In many countries like South Africa, vaccine roll-out strategies are already set in motion and have been approved following a priority group approach beginning with the most vulnerable groups, with the target being to vaccinate 67% of the population by the end of 2021.

2. Staff, "*Global survey*"

*"And I am certain that God, who began the good
work within you . . . "
(Phil 1:6)*

The story of the Prophet Jonah, a minor prophet in the Old Testament teaches us about nationalistic, racial, socio-economic differences and the ultimate mercy of God through the fulfillment of his mission—*"Why has this awful storm come down on us?" they demanded. "Who are you? What is your line of work? What country are you from? What is your nationality?"* (Jonah 1:8). God had indeed begun a *good work* within Jonah, commissioning him to be his prophet, to go to the people in the city of Nineveh, a pagan and Gentile city that had to be called to repentance. But Jonah in his reluctance decided to go the opposite direction to get away from his call of duty.

It could've been that he found this as a difficult task to do, being that he was a Hebrew going to deliver a message to the wicked Assyrians, who could've easily ended up mocking him or treating him like an utter fool. Or he probably knew that their wickedness deserved God's judgment and that preaching to them would've set them back on track, causing the Lord to relent, and this would still make him look like a fool. Whatever his reasons were, Jonah certainly did not want to do this job especially for *this* group of people.

In this fifth memory verse we find Phil 1, Paul begins by giving thanks for the church in Philippi for their hard work of spreading the Gospel of Jesus Christ, reminding them that they are doing exactly what they have been commissioned to do. It is amazing to see that God is still faithful even in our disobedience to serve him, to the point that he will rearrange everything around us, our circumstances, and sometimes even cause interruptions to our health, our lives or normal daily routine for us to yield to his calling—*"Now the Lord had arranged for a great fish to swallow Jonah. And Jonah was inside the fish for three days and three nights."* (Jonah 1:17). This shows God's mercy upon Jonah despite him wanting to flee all the way to Tarshish, a distant city thought to be towards the end of the earth. That's just how much he wanted to escape from God's appointment. But we see that even in the midst of crisis, the great storm the crewmembers experienced in the ship, Jonah never lost track of his true identity-*"I am a Hebrew, and I worship the Lord, the God of heaven, who made the sea and the land."* (Jonah 1:9).

This story is perhaps one of the reasons that gave Paul the certainty that God would finish what he started, as we see later in the book of Jonah. That even though the prophet knew that God would relent, he still managed to submit to his call eventually and carry out the task assigned to him. Jesus reminds us that we have the capacity to do this and even greater power to accomplish the works God has called us to do—*"I tell you the truth, anyone who believes in me will do the same works I have done, and even greater works, because I am going to be with the Father."* (John 14:12), and this is certainly not in our acquired human skills, but through the power of the Holy Spirit who leads gets us through our storm and mysteries, the sufferings, questions and concerns about the future—*"When the Spirit of truth comes, he will guide you into all truth. He will not speak on his own but will tell you what he has heard. He will tell you about the future."* (John 16:13).

". . . will continue his work until it is finally finished on the day when Christ Jesus returns."
(Phil 1:6)

The American novelist, Edith Wharton once wrote:

> *"There are two ways of spreading light: to be the candle or the mirror that reflects it."* [3]

In many ways, Jesus modeled discipleship to his followers while they were still together. So it wasn't hard for them understand the kind of work they were expected to do. The Gospel of John closes with this statement: *"Jesus also did many other things. If they were all written down, I suppose the whole world could not contain the books that would be written."* (John 21:25). And so it's

---

3. Wharton, *"Vesalius in Zante"*

almost impossible to imagine all the other numerous things the Lord has in store for us to do in this ministry of discipleship.

Perhaps this is where our unique talents and personalities come in. The Apostle Paul reminds us that that were are all gifted for a purpose- *"For we are God's masterpiece. He has created us anew in Christ Jesus, so we can do the good things he planned for us long ago."* (Eph 2:10). It could take a while to discover our special giftings or talents; it could even take years and years of schooling or experimenting with different jobs. However, the Apostle Paul clearly sums it up in the book of Romans—*"In his grace, God has given us different gifts for doing certain things well. So if God has given you the ability to prophesy, speak out with as much faith as God has given you. If your gift is serving others, serve them well. If you are a teacher, teach well. If your gift is to encourage others, be encouraging. If it is giving, give generously. If God has given you leadership ability, take the responsibility seriously. And if you have a gift for showing kindness to others, do it gladly."* (Rom 12:6–8).

Jesus prepared his disciples for expressing their gifts in their ministry. He further warned them that they would be faced with many troubles and persecution as they continue the good work that the Father had begun in them—*"I have told you these things so that you won't abandon your faith. For you will be expelled from the synagogues, and the time is coming when those who kill you will think they are doing a holy service for God."* (John 16:1–2).

In this instance, we ought to take courage in the fact that our obedience to Christ and our trust in him will get us through the persecution and the hatred that the world shows to the church, and gladly accept his correction and discipline when we have missed the mark. God makes us holy by his consuming fire that purifies our souls –*"For our God is a devouring fire."* (Heb 12:29). We ought to also acknowledge that he does this to prepare us, his bride so that we are spotless and blameless when He comes for us—*"Now may the God of peace make you holy in every way, and may your whole spirit and soul and body be kept blameless until our Lord Jesus Christ comes again. God will make this happen, for he who calls you is faithful."* (1 Thess 5:23–24).

Consuming Fire

"We use God's mighty weapons, not worldly weapons, to knock down the strongholds of human reasoning and to destroy false arguments"

(2 Cor 10:4)

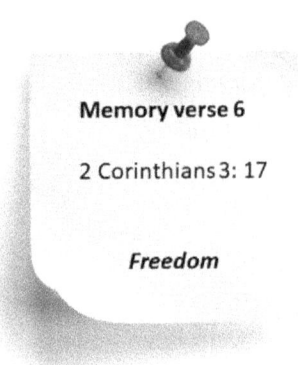

Memory verse 6

2 Corinthians 3: 17

Freedom

"For the Lord is the Spirit, and wherever the Spirit of the Lord is, there is freedom."

-2 Corinthians 3:17

Chapter 6
FREEDOM

JEHOVAH SHAMMAH IS THE Hebrew name for God meaning "The Lord is There", a name of Yahweh revealed to Ezekiel in a vision describing the ever present One who will dwell among his people in the New Jerusalem—*"The distance around the entire city will be 6 miles. And from that day the name of the city will be 'The LORD Is There."* (Ezek 48:35). Ezekiel is one of the Major Prophets in the Old Testament. His life and ministry mostly revolved around seeing visions of the Lord's glory, much like what we see in the books of Daniel and Revelation. Ezekiel prophesied to the Jewish exiles during the 70-year Babylonian invasion, along with Daniel about the future hope for Israel.

The prophet Isaiah also saw similar visions where the Lord appeared to him as *Jehovah Shammah* who revealed His glory to him—*"Attending him were mighty seraphim, each having six wings. With two wings they covered their faces, with two they covered their feet, and with two they flew. They were calling out to each other, "Holy, holy, holy is the Lord of Heaven's Armies! The whole earth is filled with his glory!" Their voices shook the Temple to its foundations, and the entire building was filled with smoke."* (Isa 6:2–4). This Temple of the Lord will exist as a complete make-over of a new world in the age to come. The Lord says *"Look! I am creating new heavens and a new earth, and no one will even think about the old ones anymore. Be glad; rejoice forever in my creation! And look! I will create Jerusalem as a place of happiness. Her people will be a source of joy."* (Isa 65:17–18).

The Apostle Paul describes the mother of faith, Sarah as the heavenly Jerusalem—*"She is the free woman, and she is our mother."* (Gal 4:26). From this expression, we note that the New Jerusalem, the Holy City of God would in fact be a city of freedom. This is the same city that our father of faith believed in—*"Abraham was confidently looking forward to a city with eternal foundations, a city designed and built by God."* (Heb 11:10). The next chapter describes the city in these terms:

> *"No, you have come to Mount Zion, to the city of the living God, the heavenly Jerusalem, and to countless thousands of angels in a joyful gathering. You have come to the assembly of God's firstborn children, whose names are written in heaven. You have come to God himself, who is the judge over all things. You have come to the spirits of the righteous ones in heaven who have now been made perfect. You have come to Jesus, the one who mediates the new covenant between God and people, and to the sprinkled blood, which speaks of forgiveness instead of crying out for vengeance like the blood of Abel."* (Heb 12:22–24).

In Rev 21, John the Apostle describes the closure of this current earth as we know it. In this instance, we see that Bible prophecy is actually quite important in Christian discipline, as it reveals a time where all of the ages known to earth finally come to an end, followed by the promise of eternity.

At present, the events recorded in the Bible would proceed with the rapture of the church, where Christ will gather all his saints, and we'll be caught up with him in the clouds and taken up to heaven to enjoy the wedding feast of the Lamb for a period of seven years (1 Thess 4:15-17), while the Great Tribulation (Jacob's trouble) takes place with the rise and rule of the antichrist on earth at the same time, until the return of Christ with the saints (Rev 6-18). Then, the battle of Armageddon will follow, fought and won by the Lord Jesus Christ himself (Rev 20:1-3), followed by His millennial reign and Satan's imprisonment for a thousand years. Next, the last rebellion against God will occur and Satan will be cast into hell for all eternity (Rev 20:7-10). Then the Great White Throne Judgment will take place, where all the Books in heaven will be open (Rev 20:11-15). And then finally, there will be an establishment of a new glorious temple in Jerusalem where God will dwell among his people in a whole new world—*"And I saw the holy city, the new Jerusalem, coming down from God out of heaven like a bride beautifully dressed for her husband."* (Rev 21:2).

In this new dwelling, *Jehovah Shammah* will live among his people as their God—*"He will wipe every tear from their eyes, and there will be no more death or sorrow or crying or pain. All these things are gone forever."* (Rev 21:3). After this, the angel of the Lord continues to reveal the bride of Christ, the church to John-*"So he took me in the Spirit to a great, high mountain, and he showed me the holy city, Jerusalem, descending out of heaven from God. It shone with the glory of God and sparkled like a precious stone—like jasper as clear as crystal. The city wall was broad and high, with twelve gates guarded by twelve angels. And the names of the twelve tribes of Israel were written on the gates. There were three gates on each side—east, north, south, and west. The wall of the city had twelve foundation stones, and on them were written the names of the twelve apostles of the Lamb."* (Rev 21:10-14).

The Lord further indicated that there would be no temple in this new city, as the one that Isaiah had probably envisioned (Isa 6:2-4), and quite different from the old one that the Israelites knew—*"I saw no temple in the city, for the Lord God Almighty and the Lamb are its temple."* (Rev 21:22). It seems that in this New Jerusalem, life will be completely different as we know it, since -*"The wolf and the lamb will feed together. The lion will eat hay like a cow. But the snakes will eat dust."* (Isa 65:25). This sounds very much like a free world, which brings us to our sixth memory verse in 2 Cor 3:17.

Fortunately, the church already has access to this kind of freedom through Christ, the Lord who lives in us—*"When I am raised to life again, you will know that I am in my Father, and you are in me, and I am in you."* (John 14:20). He spoke these words before the church was birthed pointing to his own Spirit who would later come to make his dwelling in the hearts of all believers.

In the book of Exodus, we are reminded of a significant act of God when He delivered his people from the land of Egypt. The New Year would begin with the month of their redemption. This was a fortified way of saying that 'everything is about to change.' In the emigration of the Israelites, the mystery of Passover was well established for the Jewish nation. The book clearly explains what it took for God's people to finally enjoy this celebration and what it truly meant for them. Today, we celebrate this memorial event as Easter to commemorate the death of Jesus Christ on the cross and his resurrection.

The Covid-19 pandemic may very well mimic some events that took place during the exodus of the Israelites—*"History merely repeats itself. It has all been done before. Nothing under the sun is truly new."* (Eccl 1:9). Some of the most noted epidemics in the Old Testament include the plagues that the Lord inflicted on the land of Egypt prior to the deliverance of Israel. This happened when Pharaoh kept refusing to let the Hebrews go to the wilderness to celebrate Passover.

A QUICK RECAP OF THE 10 PLAGUES OF EGYPT:

1. The river Nile turns to blood (Exod 7:20)
2. Frogs cover the whole land (Exod 8:6)
3. Swarms of gnats throughout the land cover animals and people (Exod 8:17)
4. Flies cause chaos in the whole land of Egypt, except for Goshem (Exod 8:21–22)
5. Deadly plague against livestock (Exod 9:6)
6. Festering boils break out on people and animals (Exod 9:10)
7. The worst hailstorm in Egypt's history (Exod 9:23)
8. Swarm of locusts devour crops of what's left after the hailstorm (Exod 10)
9. Thick darkness covers the land of Egypt for three days (Exod 10:22)
10. Death for Egypt's' firstborn (Exod 11)

The tenth plague describes a deadly disease that affected only certain individuals in Egypt, as a last blow of God's judgment against Pharaoh—*"On that night I will pass through the land of Egypt and strike down every firstborn son and firstborn male animal in the land of Egypt. I will execute judgment against all the gods of Egypt, for I am the Lord! But the blood on your doorposts will serve as a sign, marking the houses where you are staying. When I see the blood, I will pass over you. This plague of death will not touch you when I strike the land of Egypt."*(Exod 12:12–13).

Archaeologists have always believed that this last plague was caused by wheat infected with a fungus. But most say this seems unlikely, since infants also died and they would probably not have been eating grain by that age. Also, the fact that some children were spared, means that this plague probably went beyond scientific reasoning, and could have only been caused by God's divine intervention, much like the other nine plagues that happened miraculously. Either way, it is worth noting that this plague gave birth to a new order of worship to the Israelites, where the Lord used it to symbolize an important sacrificial offering that would eventually bring about the salvation of *all* the nations. In this way, the Lord had commanded the Israelites to celebrate Passover by first applying the blood of a lamb to the doorway of their home every year, just as it was with the death plague inflicted on Egypt. This was not only symbolic of their redemption and deliverance, but also their protection from the same death plague that the firstborn sons of the Egyptians experienced. This would then be a mark of identity for God's chosen people. We too, as the church today celebrate this by looking to the death of Jesus Christ on the Cross of Calvary as our ultimate Passover Lamb for our salvation and a mark for our redemption.

Jesus gave a splendid analogy to Nicodemus, a respected member of the Jewish council, describing what salvation meant for the Jews from the context of the Torah-*"And as Moses lifted up the bronze snake on a pole in the wilderness, so the Son of Man must be lifted up, so that everyone who believes in him will have eternal life."* (John 3:14-15). In this discussion, Jesus referred to one of the many cases where the Israelites had been complaining about their conditions and circumstances on their journey to Canaan, their promised land—*"Then the people of Israel set out from Mount Hor, taking the road to the Red Sea to go around the land of Edom. But the people grew impatient with the long journey, and they began to speak against God and Moses. "Why have you brought us out of Egypt to die here in the wilderness?" they complained. "There is nothing to eat here and nothing to drink. And we hate this horrible manna!"* (Num 21:4-5).

This complaint must have infuriated the Lord, being that He had just performed so many miraculous signs through his servant Moses right before their eyes, and yet their hearts were still hardened. And so the Lord's anger led to him sending poisonous snakes to kill the ungrateful Hebrews. After many fatalities, the people begged Moses to intercede on their behalf, which caused the Lord to relent and heal them—*"Then the Lord told him, "Make* a replica of a poisonous snake and attach it to a pole. All who are bitten will live if they simply look at it!" So Moses made a snake out of bronze and attached it to a pole. Then anyone who was bitten by a snake could look at the bronze snake and be healed!"* (Num 21:8–9). This is very much like how we believers look to Jesus Christ—Jehovah Rapha for our healing. And it's been proven to be true even when the Apostle Paul got bitten by a snake—*"But Paul shook off the snake into the fire and was unharmed."* (Acts 28:5).

"For the Lord is the Spirit . . . "
(2 Cor 3:17)

Several books in the Old Testament reveal the nature of God usually right at the end of the message that He conveys to the prophet or the priest. In the books of the Major Prophets for instance, the Lord usually seals his message off with phrases like, *"I, the Lord have spoken"* in Isaiah and Jeremiah, and *"I, the Sovereign Lord has spoken"* or *"Then you will know that I am the Lord"* in Ezekiel. When the Lord revealed himself to Moses as the *"I am"*, He said, *"Say this to the people of Israel: I am has sent me to you." God also said to Moses, "Say this to the people of Israel: Yahweh, the God of your ancestors—the God of Abraham, the God of Isaac, and the God of Jacob—has sent me to you. This is my eternal name, my name to remember for all generations.* (Exod 3:14–15). He further went deeper with the meaning of his name saying, *"I am Yahweh—'the Lord.' I appeared to Abraham, to Isaac, and to Jacob as El-Shaddai—'God Almighty'—but I did not reveal my name, Yahweh, to them."* (Exod 6:2–3). However we see that, to the twelve Minor Prophets, God revealed more about his character than merely his title:

1. *The Lord* who keeps his covenant (to Hosea)

   > *"I will be faithful to you and make you mine,*
   > *and you will finally know me as the* Lord." (Hos 2:20)

2. *The Lord* who deals with the sins of his people (to Joel)

   > *"Don't tear your clothing in your grief,*

> *but tear your hearts instead."*
> *Return to the* LORD *your God,*
> *for he is merciful and compassionate,*
> *slow to get angry and filled with unfailing love.*
> *He is eager to relent and not punish."* (Joel 2:13)

3. **The Lord God of Heaven's armies** who reveals his justice to his people (to Amos)

    > *"Instead, I want to see a mighty flood of justice,*
    > *an endless river of righteous living."* (Amos 5:24)

4. **The Lord** who reveals his justice and faithfulness to his people (to Obadiah)

    > *"Those who have been rescued will go up to Mount Zion in Jerusalem*
    > *to rule over the mountains of Edom.*
    > *And the Lord himself will be king!"* (Obad 1:21)

5. **The Lord** who is merciful (to Jonah)

    > *"But Nineveh has more than 120,000 people living in spiritual darkness, not to mention all the animals. Shouldn't I feel sorry for such a great city?"* (Jonah 4:11)

6. **The Lord** who shows compassion to his people (to Micah)

    > *"No, O people, the Lord has told you what is good,*
    > *and this is what he requires of you:*
    > *to do what is right, to love mercy,*
    > *and to walk humbly with your God."* (Mic 6:8)

7. **The Lord** who takes care of the innocent (to Nahum)

    > *"The* LORD *is good,*
    > *a strong refuge when trouble comes.*
    > *He is close to those who trust in him."* (Nah 1:7)

8. **The Eternal One** who rescues his people (to Habakkuk)

    > *"The Sovereign Lord is my strength!*

> *He makes me as surefooted as a deer,*
> *able to tread upon the heights."* (Hab 3:19)

9. *The Lord* who refines his people (to Zephaniah)

   > *"Then I will purify the speech of all people,*
   > *so that everyone can worship the Lord together."*
   > (Zeph 3:9)

10. *The Lord of glory* (to Haggai)

    > *The future glory of this Temple will be greater than its past glory, says the* LORD *of Heaven's Armies. And in this place I will bring peace. I, the Lord of Heaven's Armies, have spoken!"* (Hag 2:9)

11. *God* of revival (to Zechariah)

    > *"Not by might nor by power, but by my Spirit,' says the* LORD *Almighty."* (Zech 4:6)

12. *God* of the promise (to Malachi)

    > *"But for you who fear my name, the Sun of Righteousness will rise with healing in his wings. And you will go free, leaping with joy like calves let out to pasture."* (Mal 4:2)

Although most of these prophets may have prophesied under different circumstances, the Lord remained consistent with his character all throughout, from generation to generation-*"Jesus Christ is the same yesterday and today and forever"* (Heb 13:8); and Yahweh, who is God and King of the Jews, is the same Lord our Jewish ancestors worshipped in the wilderness, Jesus Christ himself, Yahweh—*"I the Lord do not change. So you, the descendants of Jacob, are not destroyed."* (Mal 3:6).

In this sixth memory verse, the Apostle Paul starts off by clearly stating who the Lord is. He does this by pointing to the Lord as 'the Spirit', who existed before all things came into being. The book of Genesis tells us that, *"Now the earth was formless and empty, darkness was over the surface of the deep, and the Spirit of*

FREEDOM

God was hovering over the waters." (Gen 1:2). This is the same Spirit that set life into motion -*"The Lord merely spoke, and the heavens were created."* (Ps 33:6).

It is through and *by* the Spirit that creation took place, all the stars were born, and humans came into being. It is the same Spirit that showed the prophets the visions, the same Spirit that raised Jesus Christ from the dead, the same Spirit who inspired holiness in the Old Testament -*"Teach me to do your will, for you are my God. May your gracious Spirit lead me forward on a firm footing."* (Ps 143:10). He is the same Spirit who continues to do this under the new covenant of grace—*"When the Spirit of truth comes, he will guide you into all truth. He will not speak on his own but will tell you what he has heard. He will tell you about the future."* (John 16:13). The Lord, who is the Spirit, is God's promise to Israel, that would cause them to live according to his will -*"And I will put my Spirit in you so that you will follow my decrees and be careful to obey my regulations."* (Ezek 36:27). And He is the very same Spirit who inspired David to write Psalm 91 about his promises of protection through a pandemic- *"For he will rescue you from every trap and protect you from deadly disease."*(Ps 91:3).

> "... *and wherever the Spirit of the Lord is, there is freedom."*
> *(2 Cor 3:17)*

When we consider the word 'freedom', we think of having the ability to act or do something without restraint. It is being limitless and free from any forces that confine our minds into a tiny dark box of fear or condemnation. We think of a bird that glides in the air without hindrance or the worry of falling. It is the absence of undue restrictions that only comes with being made alive in Christ -*"So if the Son sets you free, you are truly free."* (John 8:36). Freedom is to let go of all concerns of the world, to dance like David danced, to praise the Lord with shouts of 'Hallelujah!' It is to rejoice in his presence and to yield to his Holy Spirit that sometimes takes us on misunderstood adventures for the purpose of his glory, because we are his children—*"For all who are led by the Spirit of God are children of God."* (Rom 8:14–17). Freedom can be compared to having childlike faith, living in the liberty of the presence of our heavenly Father knowing and trusting that He will always take care of us no matter what. Jesus made his intentions quite clear for his followers- *"The thief's purpose is to steal and kill and destroy. My purpose is to give them a rich and satisfying life."* (John 10:10). He also prayed for our protection when he said, *"I'm not asking you to take them out of the world, but to keep them safe from the evil one."* (John 17:15), and this gives us the liberty to enjoy life.

The former president of South Africa, Nelson Mandela is a great example of a national hero who fought for this kind of freedom for his country. As an anti-apartheid activist, Mandela fought for those who were disadvantaged by the system of racial segregation, similar to the events that led to the recent movement "black lives matter" that spurred up major protests in New York amidst the coronavirus pandemic in June 2020. It seems that slavery still persists in the lives of many in the United States, only now in the form of racial policing such as the killing of George Floyd and many others by law enforcement officers, just a few months after Breonna Taylor's murder in March 2020.

In 1995, Mandela reached out to white South Africans in a grand gesture of reconciliation when he appeared at the Rugby World Cup final wearing the Springbok emblem exemplary to white supremacy in the country. It was indeed a moment celebrated as a risk-taking gesture of reconciliation when Mandela, chose to promote rugby despite the opposition he faced from his own political party. South Africa won the World Cup in the same year, and Mandela went on to establish a commission of inquiry to investigate racism and corruption in South African rugby as it seemed necessary for him to go beyond symbolism towards systemic transformation that has led to a democratic country that South Africa is today, free and liberated. In a nutshell, we see that Mandela, who had to go through a 27-year imprisonment in Robin Island to bring freedom to his country very much followed in the footsteps of the Lord Jesus Christ, who had to suffer death on the cross to bring salvation to all nations.

Freedom

The prophet Isaiah spoke this of the Messiah -*"The Spirit of the Sovereign Lord is upon me, for the Lord has anointed me to bring good news to the poor. He has sent me to comfort the brokenhearted and to proclaim that captives will be released and prisoners will be freed."* (Isa 61:1). This is what Jesus declared when he entered into his ministry to free the nation of Israel, and to bring the good news to the Gentiles, that the kingdom of God was made available to everyone.

"For you have been called to live in freedom, my brothers and sisters. But don't use your freedom to satisfy your sinful nature. Instead, use your freedom to serve one another in love."

(Gal 5:13)

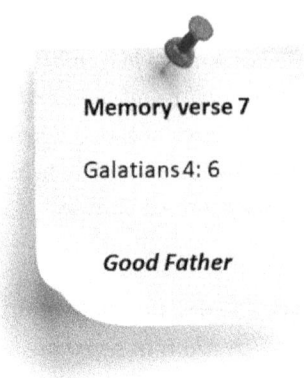

"And because we are his children, God has sent the Spirit of his Son into our hearts, prompting us to call out, "Abba, Father."

-Galatians 4: 6

Chapter 7
GOOD FATHER

JEHOVAH NISSI IS THE Hebrew name for God meaning the "The Lord is my banner". Moses was first to call upon *Jehovah Nissi* in Exod 17, when the Israelites had won a battle against the Amalekites in Rephidim. He built an altar there and named it Yahweh-Nissi (Exod 17:15). The Lord had been teaching his people how to put their trust in him just as Jesus did with his disciples during his time on earth-"*Take my yoke upon you. Let me teach you, because I am humble and gentle at heart, and you will find rest for your souls.*" (Matt 11:28).

As with most lessons, there comes a time of testing. This was seen after the Lord had displayed his miraculous wonders to both the Israelites and their Egyptian captors. He would have to test them in the wilderness to keep track of their learning process and to measure their skills to move into a higher degree of dependence on him. This would require greater faith. For the Israelites to move forward into the Promised Land, they would have to develop the right response to Yahweh's sovereignty and be made more aware of his constant and steady presence, rather than being focused on their adversity.

The nation of Israel had been delivered from 400 years of slavery and had been wandering in the desert for 40 years before making their way to the Land of Canaan. However, they always found themselves blaming their leader, Moses for their lack of sustenance, especially in the kind of arid area they found themselves in. It seems that they must have felt that they had every right to complain. Their error was that they contended with Moses, even threatening to kill him, which showed that their real problem was not only with him, but also with the Lord, despite God having provided them with manna from heaven in their previous escapade (Exod 16).

Could it be that these people were simply ungrateful, or did they just need some kind of affirmation that Yahweh hadn't deserted them *straight* after delivering them? And do *we* sometimes feel that God has deserted us when we run into troubles or get sick? No, the Lord's provision of food, rest, water, victory and wisdom in Exod 16 and 17 all point to Jesus Christ's ministry on earth, once again reminding us that He is the same Lord who sustains us—"*I am the living bread that came down from heaven. Anyone who eats this bread will live forever; and this bread, which I will offer so the world may live, is my flesh.*" (John 6:51). God proved that he would be with his people every step of the way by sending his Son Jesus, and that promise still stands today (Matt 28:20).

Before the Lord revealed himself to the Israelites as *Jehovah Nissi*, He performed yet another meaningful miracle that one would perceive to be symbolic of the wonderful gift of the Holy

Spirit that has been given to us in this present church age, who we also refer to as the Spirit of Wisdom (Eph 1:17). This prophetic event took place when the Hebrews had been thirsting for water in the scorched wilderness. They had complained so much to Moses and desperately needed to see the goodness of God. And so the Lord told Moses, *"I will stand before you on the rock at Mount Sinai. Strike the rock, and water will come gushing out. Then the people will be able to drink."* So Moses struck the rock as he was told, and water gushed out as the elders looked on." (Exod 17:6). Once again they saw God's faithfulness even in the midst of their complaining.

Today, we know that we have this water living right inside of us. So instead of worrying, complaining or pointing fingers, we can simply go straight to our heavenly Father in prayer and ask Him to open up the heavens— *"So if you sinful people know how to give good gifts to your children, how much more will your heavenly Father give the Holy Spirit to those who ask him."* (Luke 11:13).

To commemorate the events that took place during the 40-year journey of the Israelites in the wilderness, a week-long festival known as The Feast of Tabernacles is celebrated by the Jews around the month of September each year. The seventh day of the feast is considered the greatest day of the feast— *"On the last day, the climax of the festival, Jesus stood and shouted to the crowds, "Anyone who is thirsty may come to me! Anyone who believes in me may come and drink! For the Scriptures declare, 'Rivers of living water will flow from his heart."* (John 7:37-38). In this instance, we could think of Jesus as being our 'rock', who was beaten and *struck* before being crucified, and the 'rivers of living water' being his Holy Spirit—*"and all of them drank the same spiritual water. For they drank from the spiritual rock that traveled with them, and that rock was Christ."* (1 Cor 10:4).

"And because we are his children"
(Gal 4:6)

Often times we tend to forget where the Lord has brought us from, and we fall into the temptation of being overly consumed by our circumstances, which usually leaves us with very little hope for a way out. In the case of the Israelites, it seemed that the Lord brought them into the wilderness to make them realize more about who is He is and what He is able to do for his people. And at times, for us to realize God's grace, we may need to first go through hardships before we appreciate that He *will* always provide and that He *will* always make a way for us. We tend to forget this when we're in the middle of our storms and then we end up panicking. But God reminds us of his promise of provision through his prophet—*"For I am about to do something new. See, I have already begun! Do you not see it? I will make a pathway through the wilderness. I will create rivers in the dry wasteland."* (Isa 43:19).

This pandemic has caused many to fall into discouragement, usually from the negative voices around them, their peers, daily news and social media feeds. Sadness and depression then creeps up on us because of the inability to rise above these voices. It is therefore very important, now more than ever to realize that God's sovereign power and authority to get us out of these mental storms has in no way been reduced. God still uses signs and wonders to remind us that He is with us and will take care of us, much like the pillar of cloud that travelled with his people in the wilderness by day, and the pillar of fire by night, or the perhaps even the soft and gentle whisper of his Spirit in our hearts- *"Look! I stand at the door and knock. If you hear my voice and open the door, I will come in, and we will share a meal together as friends."* (Rev 3:20).

We see that in Exod 17, the Lord provided victory for his people. This is because God is always telling his people to live in faith and to repent from unbelief. Paul reminds us that, *". . . despite all these things, overwhelming victory is ours through Christ, who loved us."* (Rom 8:37).

Victory for God's people could be traced back in Israel's first war with the Amalekites, these were descendants of Esau, Jacob's brother where, *"Moses commanded Joshua, "Choose some men to go out and fight the army of Amalek for us. Tomorrow, I will stand at the top of the hill, holding the staff of God in my hand."* (Exod 17:9). As the armies lined up for battle, the men of Israel, under the command of a freshly appointed general named Joshua, could have looked up to a nearby peak and seen three figures of Moses, Aaron, and Hur standing there overlooking the battle- *"As long as Moses held up the staff in his hand, the Israelites had the advantage. But whenever he dropped his hand, the Amalekites gained the advantage."* (Exod 17:11).

For the Jews, praying with hands lifted high to God is a sign of victory. It is a posture that signifies the winning of the battle. We see that whenever Moses lifted the rod up, there was victory over the Amalekites, but when he dropped his hands low to the ground, it meant defeat. At that time, Moses wasn't a young man, so he grew tired as the battle wore on. He kept sagging and dropping his arms to his side and so immediately, the Amalekites would rally and begin to press the Israelites. But Aaron and Hur realized what was happening and stepped to Moses's side, and so they dragged a small boulder close for him to sit on and each took an arm and raised them again over the battle. As they did this, the Israelite fighters rallied to Joshua, found new strength and the Amalekites felt a new grip of fear. This caused the Israelites to win the battle— *"After the victory, the Lord instructed Moses, "Write this down on a scroll as a permanent reminder, and read it aloud to Joshua: I will erase the memory of Amalek from under heaven." Moses built an altar there and named it Yahweh-Nissi (which means "the Lord is my banner")* (Exod 17:14–15).

The Lord is indeed our banner. Banners are usually raised to celebrate honor and glory. They symbolize victory over the enemy. They hang from the rafters of arenas honoring champions and legends, soldiers returning from war. They adorn public places to celebrate occasions or people who deserve honor. They announce names and images which people can recognize from a great distance and also reveal the location and identity so people can navigate to it, and we know that we have our identity in Christ. The whole point of a banner is to be seen and unmistakable. They are intended for those who raise them and those who see them, an act of celebration, remembrance, or announcement, an invitation to a gathering place. They summon and call, and attract passers-by. This is how God, Yahweh revealed himself to be the banner for the

Israelites, *Jehovah Nissi* for all who believe, all who are His followers, all who trust Him with the same faith Moses, Aaron, Hur, and Joshua trusted. And today, He remains to be the banner for us his children—*"And I will be your Father, and you will be my sons and daughters, says the Lord Almighty"* (2 Cor 6:18).

Today, there are about 56 ongoing conflicts worldwide that have led to over 100,000 deaths in 2020 and 37,000 by April 2021. These are usually considered to be armed conflicts between at least two organized groups. They may possess a significant military involvement, and have at least a total of 100 deaths, and at least one death in the last year. The vast majority of these are insurgencies and uprisings among countries rather than big international wars, except for the recent U.S. war in Afghanistan that had been ongoing since 2001 up until August 2021, which has left many American troops killed in Kabul attacks.

At present, there are about three major wars, all of which have seen an excess of 10,000 deaths in 2020 alone and have caused many to believe that these conflicts may be linked to this current pandemic, which may perhaps also be a sign of the Lord's second coming. Jesus mentions these things in his Olivet discourse—*"And you will hear of wars and threats of wars, but don't panic. Yes, these things must take place, but the end won't follow immediately. Nation will go to war against nation, and kingdom against kingdom. There will be earthquakes in many parts of the world, as well as famines. But this is only the first of the birth pains, with more to come."* (Mark 13:7–8).

From this statement, it's not at all surprising that the end could indeed be nearer than we think since all these conflicts and plagues are taking place almost simultaneously around the globe. This, meaning that the COVID-19 pandemic could be taken as a pointer to the end of the church age according to Luke's account of the Olivet discourse—*"There will be great earthquakes, and there will be famines and plagues in many lands, and there will be terrifying things and great miraculous signs from heaven."* (Luke 21:11). Plagues in this instance could very well mean the past and present pandemics, as well as epidemics the world has witnessed thus far.

The UN Secretary-General António Guterres refers to the present COVID-19 scenario as a 'common enemy' to the world. And it sure has played out its role as just that.

The year 2020 was marked by an estimated 119,010 deaths in armed confrontations. The U.S. has described the Yemin 6-year war as the "worst humanitarian crisis in the world" in 2019, with hostilities having directly caused tens of thousands of civilian casualties in the first nine months of 2020, and nearly a quarter of a million deaths. The Tigray war, also an ongoing conflict that began in 2020, has killed over 17,000 people and has left more than 50,000 Ethiopians displaced to Sudan. The Boko Haram insurgence entered its tenth year of conflict despite increased security measures in 2019, having claimed over 8,200 lives in 2020 spanning across different African countries. There's also been the ongoing conflict between Israel and Palestine known to be one of the most enduring conflicts, having lasted around 54 years with various attempts being made to resolve it. And the question remains, when will this all ever come to an end?

The Lord however does remind us that despite all the Christian persecution happening around the world, it is not yet the end. This is because we are expected to go through these trials as believers of Christ, and so it should be of no surprise that Christians are being killed, martyred or imprisoned to this day, as they did in the days of the Apostles in the early church. We are of no less God's children now than the first believers were 2,000 years ago—"*But this is the new covenant I will make with the people of Israel on that day, says the Lord: I will put my laws in their minds, and I will write them on their hearts. I will be their God, and they will be my people.*" (Heb 8:10).

We also know that those who suffer persecution for Christ's sake, like most of the Apostles *will* be raised up on the last day. Paul said this, "*For I fully expect and hope that I will never be ashamed, but that I will continue to be bold for Christ, as I have been in the past. And I trust that my life will bring honor to Christ, whether I live or die. For to me, living means living for Christ, and dying is even better.*" (Phil 1:20–21).

For Peter, Jesus warned him about the kind of death he would be faced with- *"I tell you the truth, when you were young, you were able to do as you liked; you dressed yourself and went wherever you wanted to go. But when you are old, you will stretch out your hands, and others will dress you and take you where you don't want to go."* (John 21:18). We are all unique and have different stories of our journey with Christ, and so we may differ in our God-defined calling. Nevertheless, it remains clearly undeniable that Christian persecution is inevitable. And thank God that Jesus promised that he would not abandon us in the midst of it all- *"No, I will not abandon you as orphans—I will come to you."* (John 14:18).

"*. . . God has sent the Spirit of his Son into our hearts*"
(Gal 4:6)

The book of Isaiah reveals many of the Lord's promises for his people, the nation of Israel, one of them being the promised Messiah, Jesus Christ through the line of Jesse (Isa 52–53), as well as the seven-fold Spirit of God that the saints inherit through Christ-*"And the Spirit of the Lord will rest on him—the Spirit of wisdom and understanding, the Spirit of counsel and might, the Spirit of knowledge and the fear of the Lord."* (Isa 11:2). This is the work of the Holy Spirit who dwells only in those who believe and belong to Jesus Christ—*"So I want you to know that no one speaking by the Spirit of God will curse Jesus, and no one can say Jesus is Lord, except by the Holy Spirit."* (1 Cor 12:3). He is our guarantee to inherit salvation—*"But when the Father sends the Advocate as my representative—that is, the Holy Spirit—he will teach you everything and will remind you of everything I have told you."* (John 14:26). And because the Holy Spirit dwells in us, we can function like Christ on whilst here earth because we have inherited his mind and perceptions, and not the world view of the things happening around us -*"For, "Who can know the Lord's thoughts? Who knows enough to teach him?" But we understand these things, for we have the mind of Christ."* (1 Cor 2:16). So since we have the mind of

Christ, doesn't that make us function more like him in the daily challenges we face?

> "... prompting us to call out, "Abba, Father."
> (Gal 4:6)

We know that because we believe in our Lord Jesus who is the Son of God, we have also been adopted into his royal family and we share in the same inheritance that he received from the Father—"So don't boast about following a particular human leader. For everything belongs to you— whether Paul or Apollos or Peter, or the world, or life and death, or the present and the future. Everything belongs to you, and you belong to Christ, and Christ belongs to God." (1 Cor 3:21–23). We are now children of God through our faith in Christ through the Holy Spirit that God has sent into our hearts. He is the same Spirit who reveals Christ to us and the inheritance that God has given to us—"No one can know a person's thoughts except that person's own spirit, and no one can know God's thoughts except God's own Spirit. And we have received God's Spirit (not the world's spirit), so we can know the wonderful things God has freely given us." (1 Cor 2:11–12).

But what is so significant about calling our heavenly Father 'Abba Father'? Can't we just simply call Him 'our Father' like everybody else? Or refer to Him the same way Jesus taught his disciples to pray (the Lord's Prayer)? Well, it seems that this comes with a deeper walk of faith to claim the same intimate relationship that Jesus Christ had with his Abba.

'Abba' is an Aramaic term for father. Jesus referred to the Father this way to point out his intimacy with Him on the cross right before his crucifixion—"Abba, Father," he cried out, "everything is possible for you. Please take this cup of suffering away from me. Yet I want your will to be done, not mine." (Mark 14:36). And this is how we ought to imitate him in our daily walk of faith, for the Lord's will to be done over our desires. Our heavenly Father loves us dearly, like a father loves his children. Many orphans and fatherless children would not be able to completely perceive this kind of love. However, we can always look to the cross to understand how Abba Father loved his Son Jesus, and this is exactly how He loved the world, that He sacrificed his own Son to give *us* eternal life (John 3:16).

Since everything belongs to us as God's children, we can only take pride in the fact that we are indeed his children. Paul puts it this way, *"Therefore, as the Scriptures say, "If you want to boast, boast only about the Lord."* (1 Cor 1:31). Later he reminds the church in Corinth that death is inevitable, it is unavoidable—*"For I swear, dear brothers and sisters, that I face death daily. This is as certain as my pride in what Christ Jesus our Lord has done in you."* (1 Cor 15:31). And so we boast in the Lord by calling out the name of our Lord, *Jehovah Nissi!* Yes, He will give us victory over every battle. He will resurrect our mortal bodies, He will heal us of infirmity, because He is our banner, and in him we will put our trust forever—*"We do this by keeping our eyes on Jesus, the champion who initiates and perfects our faith. Because of the joy awaiting him, he endured the cross, disregarding its shame. Now he is seated in the place of honor beside God's throne."* (Heb 12:2). He is the One who wears the Victor's crown, the crown of thorns for his victory over death on the Cross—*"And they sang in a mighty chorus: "Worthy is the Lamb who was slaughtered—to receive power and riches and wisdom and strength and honor and glory and blessing."* (Rev 5:12). Amen.

Victor's Crown

Then Jesus came out wearing the crown of thorns and the purple robe.
And Pilate said, "Look, here is the man!"

-John 19:15

"So you have not received a spirit that makes you fearful slaves. Instead, you received God's Spirit when he adopted you as his own children. Now we call him, "Abba, Father."

(Rom 8:15)

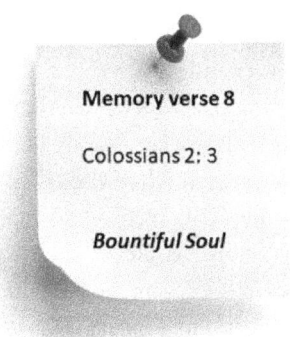

Memory verse 8

Colossians 2: 3

Bountiful Soul

"In him lie hidden all the treasures of wisdom and knowledge."

-Colossians 2:3

Chapter 8
Bountiful Soul

JEHOVAH 'ORI IS THE Hebrew name for God meaning the "Lord is my Light" taken from David's Psalm—*"The LORD is my light and my salvation—so why should I be afraid?"* (Ps 27:1). This speaks of the troubles David usually faced with his adversaries and false witnesses, violent men and pretty much his enemies that eagerly wanted him dead, much like king Saul who persistently hunted him down with reckless abandon. David took comfort in knowing that *Jehovah 'Ori* would light up his dark paths in the midst of the dark valleys that he had to go through. The Lord would surely protect him, guide him, surround him with his presence and save him from the wrath of his enemies.

Right in the beginning of Ps 27 we see that David describes Jehovah's character as light. But what exactly could this mean for the world in this perilous season when there's so much going on and everything seems so bleak? It even seems that this plague has blinded the vision of so many people, as the Prophet Isaiah put it—*"Darkness as black as night covers all the nations of the earth, but the glory of the Lord rises and appears over you."* (Isa 60:2). In this verse, the glory of the Lord that Isaiah speaks of, may very well be reckoned with the same light that David was referring to in Ps 27. Visible light as we know it is some form of radiation that can be detected by the human eye. Without light, nothing can be seen. It is like walking into a dark room, having your eyes shut or blindfolded. There is no visible image produced, except if you light a candle. When the glory of the Lord rises and appears over a person, it can be detected by the fruit that is produced in their lives—*"In the same way, let your good deeds shine out for all to see, so that everyone will praise your heavenly Father."* (Matt 5:16).

The phrase *"Let there be light"* comes from Gen 1:3, where in the beginning of creation, all that existed was a formless and empty earth, and darkness covered the deep waters. Light was the first thing that God ever made that paved a way to all his other creations including the sky, the land, vegetation, animals and humans. Light could also be taken as the source that sparks up our imagination, our understanding of things, divine revelation and deeper truths about God's mysteries concerning our lives -*"The teaching of your word gives light, so even the simple can understand."* (Ps 119:140). In this sense, light comes when we look into the Holy Bible, the living Word of God. The Lord reveals truths from his Word that our minds may have forgotten, or things that we have never heard of or understood especially in complex situations where there is no clear answer to what we ought to do.

Many times we tend to misunderstand other believers even in our own circles. We are quick to pass judgments simply because we don't understand what they are talking about. And so, it is only through God's Word that we gain better understanding of why things happen, why someone said something that did not sit well with us, and why the Lord places us in these circumstances. This eighth memory verse in Col 2:3, is a reminder that it is only through the Word of God that we will find answers to most our questions in this life. Here, the Apostle Paul pours his heart out to the Christians in the church of Colossae as well as all the other believers he had never met personally and says, *"I want them to be encouraged and knit together by strong ties of love. I want them to have complete confidence that they understand God's mysterious plan, which is Christ himself. In him lie hidden all the treasures of wisdom and knowledge."* (Col 2:2–3). And we know that the Word of God, who is Jesus Christ, is the one who gives us internal light to reveal these hidden treasures.

John 1:1–5
"In the beginning the Word already existed.
The Word was with God,
and the Word was God.
He existed in the beginning with God.
God created everything through him,
and nothing was created except through him.
The Word gave life to everything that was created,
and his life brought light to everyone.
The light shines in the darkness,
and the darkness can never extinguish it"

In one of his parables, Jesus likened his second coming to a story of ten virgins waiting for the bridegroom to come for the wedding feast (Matt 25). All ten of the virgins had fallen asleep because the bridegroom was delayed. However, the other five, though asleep, were ready for his coming, having carried extra oil to last them until his arrival. According to Tim MacWelch, an author of some several outdoor survival books, *any* kind of oil can be used to light up a lamp to survive out in the wilderness. He stated this in one of his blogs:

> *"I have been a fanatical user of primitive lighting for years now, especially on campouts and in teaching survival classes. I've learned over the years that with the proper wick (plant fiber) and any oil, you can make an oil lamp. Liquid or solid oil—animal, vegetable or mineral—all are effective in making grease lamps and oil "candles."* [1]

Christ's parable in Matt 25 on the other hand speaks of olive oil specifically, not just *any* other oil. This must be a special kind of oil that all believers would need to be well prepared for Christ's return. In this context, olive oil represents the Holy Spirit, who works hand in hand with Christ in our hearts—*"When the Spirit of truth comes, he will guide you into all truth. He will not speak on his own but will tell you what he has heard. He will tell you about the future."* (John 16:13). This could only mean that the Holy Spirit has to hear from the Lord to convey a message that sheds light and insight to our souls. And so, if the 'wise virgins' carry enough of this kind of anointing, they will do everything necessary to have enough of it to keep their lamps burning until the bridegroom makes his way for the wedding —*"At midnight they were roused by the shout, 'Look, the bridegroom is coming! Come out and meet him!'"* (Matt 25:6).

It makes it almost impossible to separate light and the olive oil spoken of in this parable, as they clearly work together to prepare us for the Lord's return, and we know that Jesus is the Light we are seeking for, the Light we pursue daily and the Light that will lead us home to be with our heavenly Father. Jesus says, *"I am the light of the world. If you follow me, you won't have to walk in darkness, because you will have the light that leads to life."* (John 8:12). The olive oil used in the parable serves as fuel to light up the lamp for the night. But olive oil could also serve other purposes for these virgins; to heal their wounds in case of any unprecedented accidents or sickness, or to provide warmth and comfort while waiting for the bridegroom.

The Hebrew word for 'olive tree' is *es shemen*, which literally means 'tree of oil'. It is from a primitive root meaning 'to shine.'

1. MacWelch, *"Survival skills"*

It also means richness, anointing, ointment or olive. It is related to the Hebrew word *shemesh, which means* 'to be brilliant' which sometimes refers to the brilliance of the Lord's splendor, the Lord's glory -"*He held seven stars in his right hand, and a sharp two-edged sword came from his mouth. And his face was like the sun in all its brilliance.*" (Rev 1:16). This kind of brilliance offered by the Lord's anointing is often seen in people who possess life and abundant joy in them, a bountiful soul— "*You love him even though you have never seen him. Though you do not see him now, you trust him; and you rejoice with a glorious, inexpressible joy.*" (1 Pet 1:8). This kind of joy is mostly seen in many charismatic churches, where there's exuberant and highly elevated praise and worship, non-stop clapping, random shouts of 'Hallelujah!' and cheerful, joyful singing and dancing. This follows the words of the Apostle Paul who said, "*Always be full of joy in the Lord. I say it again—rejoice! Let everyone see that you are considerate in all you do. Remember, the Lord is coming soon.*" (Phil 4:4).

The olive tree was one of the most valuable trees to the ancient Hebrews, first mentioned in Genesis when the dove had returned to Noah's ark carrying an olive branch in its beak after the flood— "*After waiting another seven days, Noah released the dove again. This time the dove returned to him in the evening with a fresh olive leaf in its beak.*" (Gen 8:11). Since that time, the olive branch has been a symbol of 'peace' to the world, which also relates to the dove, symbolic of the presence of the Holy Spirit—"*After his baptism, as Jesus came up out of the water, the heavens were opened and he saw the Spirit of God descending like a dove and settling on him.*" (Matt 3:16).

When Israel conquered Canaan, the olive tree was a noticeable feature among the flora of the land. This was the land of the Promise described as, "*a land of wheat and barley; of grapevines, fig trees, and pomegranates; of olive oil and honey*" (Deut 8:8). The olive was a very important source of income to the early Israelites. It was tithed upon along with all the produce of the land (Deut 12:17). God further told Moses regarding Aaron, "*Then anoint him by pouring the anointing oil over his head.*" (Exod 29:7) as a way to portray the leadership anointing that had been laid upon his life. The Tabernacle, the Ark of the Covenant, the Table of Showbread, the Lampstand, the Altar, the Laver, and its foot, were all anointed with the same precious compound, as a holy oil of anointing (Exod 30:26–33), which was also used to anoint the daily sacrifices. The lampstand in the Tabernacle was with the 'oil for the light' with its seven lamps—*"Command the people of Israel to bring you pure oil of pressed olives for the light, to keep the lamps burning continually"* (Lev 24:2).

Clearly from the parable of the ten virgins, olive oil is a key component in the kingdom of heaven. The Old Testament tells us that the lack of having this is often associated with a curse. One of the curses of disobedience was to suffer great loss or to perish— *"You will plant crops but not harvest them. You will press your olives but not get enough oil to anoint yourselves. You will trample the grapes but get no juice to make your wine."* (Mic 6:16). We note this with the five foolish virgins who did not have enough oil to sustain them—*"Later, when the other five bridesmaids returned, they stood outside, calling, 'Lord! Lord! Open the door for us!' "But he called back, 'Believe me, I don't know you!'* (Matt 25:11–12).

> *"In him lie hidden all the treasures of wisdom . . . "*
> (Col 2:3)

This parable of the ten virgins indicates that there are some who know Jesus, who may even pray using the name of Jesus, who've been brought up in a Jesus-centered church, and yet actually, do not know him at all —*"On judgment day many will say to me, 'Lord! Lord! We prophesied in your name and cast out demons in your name and performed many miracles in your name.' But I will reply, 'I never knew you. Get away from me, you who break God's laws.'"* (Matt 7:22–23). This will happen because these disciples didn't have a real relationship with Christ. They lacked the special ingredient, the fuel for their light, the anointing, or the olive oil, the Holy Spirit. The Holy Spirit is the key to our final redemption. Without him, the light we have is actually not light at all. This may be the exact same reason why David pleaded with the Lord in his prayer of repentance -"*Do not banish me from your presence, and don't take your Holy Spirit from me.*" (Ps 51:11). He knew how important it was to function with the Lord's anointing. God's Spirit illuminates truth about his laws and commandments -"*You love justice and hate evil. Therefore God, your God, has anointed you, pouring out the oil of joy on you more than on anyone else.*" (Ps 45:7). This could point to the idea that oil is also symbolic of purity and joy, as with the 'joy' being one of the fruit produced in us by the Holy Spirit (Gal 5:22–23).

In this present pandemic, it seems that many of the light-bearers have been silenced either by sickness from the virus or the effects of the pandemic. There is widespread recognition that this coronavirus is far more unpredictable than any other simple respiratory virus. The SARS-CoV-2 known to be the seed of the coronavirus family, is so severe that it spreads before people show any symptoms of the disease and has made it even more difficult to control, apart from the social distance measures that the different governments have put in place and the new vaccines that were quickly approved by the FDA. Trying to define this pathogen in the midst of an ever-spreading pandemic has also posed difficulties with claims from scientists that say it could take several years to fully understand how the disease damages organs and how medications, genetics, diets, lifestyles and distancing impact its course.

As we know, the virus often attacks the lungs, but it can also strike anywhere from the brain to the toes, beginning only with a few symptoms or sometimes none at all; then days later, squeeze the air out of the lungs without warning. It targets men and women alike, the elderly, and immunosuppressed people. Coronavirus, with its variants-alpha, beta, delta and now novel ones, attacks the heart, savages the kidneys to such an extent that some hospitals have run short of dialysis equipment. It makes its way along the nervous system, destroying taste and smell and occasionally reaching the brain, and creates sudden blood clots, inflaming blood vessels throughout the body. This is a serious plague that has caused many deaths in the world.

The KFF analysis data from the Census Bureau's Household Pulse survey (an ongoing survey created to capture data on health and economic impacts of the pandemic) shows the prevalence of mental illness and related disorders that have occurred during the COVID-19 pandemic. It basically reveals how drastically these mental disorders and substance abuse have increased since the beginning of the pandemic. In January 2021, 41% adults were reported symptoms of anxiety and/or depressive disorder related to coronavirus-related stress, as well as reported thoughts of suicide that seem to be worsening as the pandemic progressed. Earlier data from 2020 shows that drug overdose deaths were particularly pronounced from March to May 2020, around the same time the lockdowns were put in place[2]. This of course caused many sadness and sorrow in the eyes of believers, who've been limited in expressing the light that shines in them. It is only through the work of the Holy Spirit that passion and hope to live can be restored again — *"But you are not like that, for you are a chosen people. You are royal priests, a holy nation, God's very own possession. As a result, you can show others the goodness of God, for he called you out of the darkness into his wonderful light."* (1 Pet 2:9).

Jehovah Ezer, meaning 'The Lord is our helper' is a Hebrew phrase that adds on to the main function of the Holy Spirit, who is the oil that we need to keep our light ablaze. He is our helper, our teacher and our advocate who pleads to the Father for us on our behalf (John 14:26). He is the Spirit of Wisdom—*"But it was to us that God revealed these things by his Spirit. For his Spirit searches out everything and shows us God's deep secrets"* (1 Cor 2:10). By God's grace, most people have recovered from Covid-19 and have managed to build immunity from the disease, while others have gone on ahead to rest until Christ returns to take us all home—*"Good people pass away; the godly often die before their time. But no one seems to care or wonder why. No one seems to understand that God is protecting them from the evil to come. For those who follow godly paths will rest in peace when they die."* (Isa 57:1–2).

---

2. Panchal et al, *"The implications of COVID-19 for mental health"*, 21

And for those who survive the sickness, who remain alive today, things will take on a new turn. We will need to truly reflect on this crisis, and draw lessons from it, seek God's counsel impart these truths to those around us and those that follow after us - *"If you need wisdom, ask our generous God, and he will give it to you. He will not rebuke you for asking."* (Jas 1:5). In essence, asking God for wisdom is asking Him to reveal his ways of solving issues in complex predicaments through gained knowledge from experience as in this instance. This will often lead us into having to go through our own personal life crises, or living through a pandemic such as COVID-19, which happens to be a on a much larger scale, so that we get the chance to grow and experience God's ways and acquire godly wisdom.

The Lord does not rebuke us for asking for wisdom. He will give to us what we ask for, and perhaps take us through a pandemic that affects the whole world so that we don't feel all alone in this battle. He will give us a tale for us to tell to future generations, just as he did with the Israelites and the Apostles, and those that that he has healed and delivered in the past, including all the survivors of this present pandemic. We've all got a story to tell from all the lessons that have taught us God's wisdom—*"But the wisdom from above is first of all pure. It is also peace loving, gentle at all times, and willing to yield to others. It is full of mercy and the fruit of good deeds. It shows no favoritism and is always sincere."* (Jas 3:17). This is truly how the church is being sanctified in the midst this pandemic, to gain true knowledge of the Holy One.

Proverbs 2:2-6
"Tune your ears to wisdom,
and concentrate on understanding.
Cry out for insight,
and ask for understanding.
Search for them as you would for silver;
seek them like hidden treasures.
Then you will understand what it means to fear
the Lord,
and you will gain knowledge of God.
For the Lord grants wisdom!
From his mouth come knowledge and understanding."

> *"In him lie hidden all the hidden treasures of . . . knowledge."*
> *(Col 2:3)*

The Apostle Paul states that, *"For God, who said, "Let there be light in the darkness," has made this light shine in our hearts so we could know the glory of God that is seen in the face of Jesus Christ."* (2 Cor 4:6). For the light to shine in those dark places of unfamiliarity, knowledge is needed. From Isaiah's prophecy concerning the seven-fold Spirit that would rest upon the Messiah (Isa 11:2), we also see that the treasures found in the Lord come with the Spirit of knowledge. This could also be taken as a spiritual gift given to certain individuals in the church- *"A spiritual gift is given to each of us so we can help each other. To one person the Spirit gives the ability to give wise advice; to another the same Spirit gives a message of special knowledge."* (1 Cor 12:7-8).

Knowledge is acquired in different ways, from perception, reason, memory, education, experience or through personal testimony. With knowledge comes learning and understanding that we often put into practice or apply to our circumstances. Paul prayed, *"May you experience the love of Christ, though it is too great to understand fully. Then you will be made complete with all the fullness of life and power that comes from God."* (Eph 3:19). In his petition under Roman imprisonment and chained to a Roman solider, Paul made this prayer especially for the Gentiles in Ephesus, that they would experience or have the full knowledge about Christ's love despite it being too hard for our minds to comprehend. His point was that to come to any kind of understanding of the dimensions of God's love, we *need* to come to the Cross to experience his suffering, to know him and to be made wise—*"Look, I am sending you out as sheep among wolves. So be as shrewd as snakes and harmless as doves."* (Matt 10:16).

> *"For once you were full of darkness, but now you have light from the Lord. So live as people of light!"*
>
> (Eph 5:8)

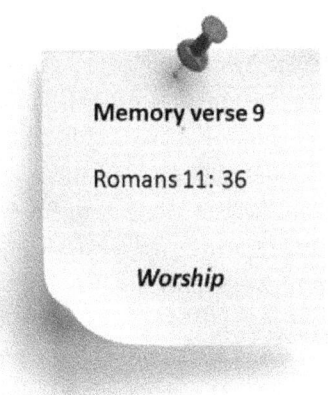

"For everything comes from him and exists by his power and is intended for his glory. All glory to him forever! Amen."

-Romans 11:36

Chapter 9
Worship

JEHOVAH SABAOTH IS THE Hebrew name for God meaning, "The Lord of Heaven's armies" or "The Lord of hosts", first mentioned in 1 Sam 1:3 where Elkanah, Samuel's father would travel to Shiloh to worship the Lord and offer sacrifices to him at the Tabernacle. This name of the Lord denotes his universal sovereignty over all the hosts and armies, both in the spiritual and the earthly realm. He *is* the Lord God Almighty, El-Shaddai, *Jehovah*, and the ever-existing

One who reveals himself unceasingly. As with all the heavenly beings are called hosts, *Jehovah* is the Lord of this host revealing himself as is their Maker and Governor, their King and Ruler, and that He alone is the proper object of their affection and worship. *Jehovah Sabaoth* is God's name to indicate his all-powerful authority to create, to build up, to tear down, to destroy, to heal, to sustain, and to cut-off, just as He did with some of the angels like Lucifer who was cast down from heaven along with his servants—*"This great dragon—the ancient serpent called the devil, or Satan, the one deceiving the whole world—was thrown down to the earth with all his angels."* (Rev 12:9).

Jehovah Sabaoth is God's name of man's extremities. We see that when one of Elkanah's wives, Hannah had been deeply depressed about not having any children, she wept bitterly after being severely taunted and being made fun of year in and year out by another of Elkanah's wives, Peninah who *did* have children with him. Hannah found herself in an extreme condition where the only way out was to call upon *Jehovah Sabaoth* to fight her battle of being barren and continually harassed—*"And she made this vow: "O Lord of Heaven's Armies, if you will look upon my sorrow and answer my prayer and give me a son, then I will give him back to you."* (1 Sam 1:11). This name of the Lord unravels God's transcend nature, that He goes beyond the limits of our imaginations. He is a supernatural God whose miracles surpass all scientific knowledge or human reasoning, for we know that, *"What is impossible for people is possible with God."* (Luke 18:27). This is why He alone is *Jehovah Sabaoth*. He is omnipresent, present everywhere at all times; omnipotent, all-powerful and majestic; and He is the omniscient God who knows all things and made all things.

In the battle between a young David and his adversary, the great Goliath, David related to this character of the Lord -*"David replied to the Philistine, "You come to me with sword, spear, and javelin, but I come to you in the name of the Lord of Heaven's Armies—the God of the armies of Israel, whom you have defied"* (1 Sam 17:45). David, after having killed a bear and a lion with his own bare hands had become much aware that every battle and conflict he had faced wasn't his, but belonged to the Lord. David knew that being in the presence of the Lord, would nullify all his troubles—*"The one thing I ask of the Lord—the thing I seek most—is to live in the house of the Lord all the days of my life, delighting in the Lord's perfections and meditating in his Temple"* (Ps 27:4). By him referring to the Lord as the Lord of heaven's armies, David was simply alluding to the Lord's strength, his awesomeness and his divine character that is capable of overcoming anything and everything. This positioned David's heart for the Lord to manifest his victory over Goliath.

Two of the Major Prophets, Isaiah and Jeremiah also referred to Jehovah by this name. They'd have to *really* depend on *Jehovah Sabaoth* to overcome the resistance they had faced with the people of Israel, while they ever-so-often had to present doom and gloom prophecies about the coming judgment of the Lord against this nation. But despite the disaster that was to come upon them, the prophets always reminded the people that, *"Our Redeemer, whose name is the Lord of Heaven's Armies, is the Holy One of Israel"* (Isa 47:4), and He would fight for them against their captors and win their wars against their enemies.

The 'hosts' of armies in heaven includes the angels and all the heavenly creatures we read about in the prophet's visions such as those seen by Isaiah, Daniel, Ezekiel and the Apostle John in the book of Revelation. Jesus is the Lord over all these armies—*"Then I saw heaven opened, and a white horse was standing there. Its rider was named Faithful and True, for he judges fairly and wages a righteous war. His eyes were like flames of fire, and on his head were many crowns. A name was written on him that no one understood except himself. He wore a robe dipped in blood, and his title was the Word of God. The armies of heaven, dressed in the finest of pure white linen, followed him on white horses."* (Rev 19:11–14).

There's also several other supernatural beings that exist which we cannot see with the physical eye that the Apostle Paul refers to in his letter to the church in Ephesus—*"For we are not fighting against flesh-and-blood enemies, but against evil rulers and authorities of the unseen world, against mighty powers in this dark world,* and against evil spirits in the heavenly places." (Eph 6:12). And so we fight this war through prayer—*"Pray in the Spirit at all times and on every occasion. Stay alert and be persistent in your prayers for all believers everywhere."* (Eph 6:18). These mighty powers we are waging war against exist only in invisible realities. They include demons, or unclean spirits that are able to enter human bodies and take possession of them or oppress people—totally different from God's angels, who are known to be ministering spirits who serve the Lord by helping his people—*"See, I am sending an angel before you to protect you on your journey and lead you safely to the place I have prepared for you."* (Exod 23:20). We also see this when Jesus was tested in the wilderness for 40 days and 40 nights without any food—*"Then the devil left him, and angels came and attended him."* (Matt 4:11).

Angels are entities under God's control—*"Therefore, angels are only servants—spirits sent to care for people who will inherit salvation."* (Heb 1:14); they also serve to minister in heaven serving God in constant worship—*"And all the angels were standing around the throne and around the elders and the four living beings. And they fell before the throne with their faces to the ground and worshiped God."* (Rev 7:11). Angels serve many other duties as they will play a big role in the final judgment of destroying this earth as we know it—*"Then I saw four angels standing at the four corners of the earth, holding back the four winds so they did not blow on the earth or the sea, or even on any tree. And I saw another angel coming up from the east, carrying the seal of the living God. And he shouted to those four angels, who had been given power to harm land and sea, "Wait! Don't harm the land or the sea or the trees until we have placed the seal of God on the foreheads of his servants."* (Rev 7:1–3).

"For everything comes from him . . . "
(Rom 11:36)

Several biblical scholars consider Job to be the oldest book of the Old Testament, probably belonging to the period covered by the book of Genesis, around the time of Abraham. Its lessons are therefore one of the oldest and probably most crucial we can apply

WORSHIP

in today's pandemic. Job is regarded to be the earliest of all written accounts about the origin of disease. The book tells a story about a righteous man named Job, who greatly feared the Lord and held an impeccable reputation and wealth among his people. We read later that he often did good for others, he rescued the needy, cared personally for the handicapped and the dying, brought orphans into his home and even took the influence of his day to court to argue the cases for the underprivileged.

In the first chapter of the book, a scene in heaven is revealed, where the devil is first mentioned as the Accuser—*"One day the members of the heavenly court came to present themselves before the Lord, and the Accuser, Satan, came with them. "Where have you come from?" the Lord asked Satan."* (Job 1:6-7). Satan, submitting to the Lord's authority answers and tells him that he's been patrolling the earth and watching everything that's going on. It seems that the Lord used Satan as an instrument to prove a point about his faithful servants, including Job. We see that Satan wasn't prepared to back down from this, he wanted a challenge. And so God allowed Satan to test Job—*"Satan replied to the Lord, "Skin for skin! A man will give up everything he has to save his life. But reach out and take away his health, and he will surely curse you to your face!"* (Job 2:4). However, we see that Job never gave in. He kept his loyalty even after being tested by his wife to give up—*"His wife said to him, "Are you still trying to maintain your integrity? Curse God and die."* (Job 2:9).

After Job's first test, Satan once again went to the heavenly court. It's almost as if Satan had been put on trial for accusing the righteous, hence he was always appearing before God with the other angels. This is probably the reason he is known as the 'Accuser'. John described him this way, *"For the accuser of our brothers and sisters has been thrown down to earth—the one who accuses them before our God day and night."* (Rev 12:10). The brothers and sisters spoken of by John are the believers who are righteous just like Job, through faith in Christ Jesus, which is the church. As is written, *"And my righteous ones will live by faith. But I will take no pleasure in anyone who turns away."* (Heb 10:38). We see that Job did *not* turn away, he kept his righteousness amidst the calamity, loss, discouragement, confusion, sickness and depression that he had to go through. He was sure enough to maintain his faith without falling into Satan's traps.

Another lesson we can take from Job's story is that sickness and disease are in fact caused by Satan, but are allowed by God— *"So Satan left the Lord's presence, and he struck Job with terrible boils from head to foot"* (Job 2:7). God grants Satan permission to test us with infirmity and affliction, just as He did when he used King Nebuchadnezzar and Pharaoh as instruments to punish Israel. And so everything *does* come from the Lord, as we see in this ninth memory verse in Rom 11:36, because later in the book of Job, we see that, *"God disciplines people with pain on their sickbeds, with ceaseless aching in their bones. They lose their appetite for even the most delicious food. Their flesh wastes away, and their bones stick out."* (Job 33:19–21).

And we know that the Lord's discipline is sometimes exactly what we need to turn away from sin, to slow us down from the fast pace of life, and to ground ourselves back into his love — *"The Lord disciplines everyone he loves. He severely disciplines everyone he accepts as his child."* (Heb 12:6). In this way, we can always be thankful, even in our infirmities, because we know that it is all out of God's love for us. Paul says, *"We can rejoice, too, when we run into problems and trials, for we know that they help us develop endurance. And endurance develops strength of character, and character strengthens our confident hope of salvation. And this hope will not lead to disappointment. For we know how dearly God loves us, because he has given us the Holy Spirit to fill our hearts with his love."* (Rom 5:3–4).

> *". . . and exists by his power and is intended for his glory"*
> *(Rom 11:36)*

It comes with no doubt that the coronavirus pandemic exits, we can all attest to this although some people are still in denial about it for some reason or the other. Unfortunately, as dramatic as it has played out so far, it's not a film. It *is* in fact all around us and has killed millions of people. By early September 2021, an estimated 4.5 million global deaths were reported, with over 200 million active cases of the disease, since its first appearance in December 2019. Much like the 1918 influenza pandemic that took at least 50 million lives in the previous century, coronavirus cases are still on the rise.

Now, could this disease be all for God's glory?

Well, according to this memory verse in Rom 11:36, we see that *everything* does indeed exist for the glory of God. When Jesus had been posed with a similar question by his disciples about why a certain beggar had been blind from birth, he simply told them that it had nothing to do with his sins or his parents' but, *"This happened so the power of God could be seen in him."* (John 9:3). For this reason, Jesus healed this man's eyes and he could finally see, and this surely gave glory to God.

We see that throughout the Bible, for God's power to be displayed, something had to change, there often had to be a shaking that required God's intervention, and the same goes for what we are experiencing today—*"For the Lord of Heaven's Armies has a day of reckoning. He will punish the proud and mighty and bring down everything that is exalted"* (Isa 2:12). There still remains a dire need for the world to be saved, and perhaps what the world needs is a wake-up call, a deep sense of urgency to repent, to seek the Lord, and for the Saints to present the Father to the world that is in desperate need of him—*"Pray this way for kings and all who are in authority so that we can live peaceful and quiet lives marked by godliness and dignity. This is good and pleases God our Savior, who wants everyone to be saved and to understand the truth."* (1 Tim 2:2-4).

There is simply no other deity or religion, hobby or career, person or anything else that people hold dear to that could ever replace the reality of the truth about Christ. For light to come, there first has to be darkness, and perhaps this pandemic presents itself as a platform for the world to acknowledge the darkness that surrounds us, so that the church can manifest the light of God-*"No one lights a lamp and then puts it under a basket. Instead, a lamp is placed on a stand, where it gives light to everyone in the house. In the same way, let your good deeds shine out for all to see, so that everyone will praise your heavenly Father"* (Matt 5:15-16). And Psalm 66 is a perfect example of how David praised the Lord in the midst of his trials, reflecting on his goodness in the past and rejoicing in unfailing love for his people.

> *"All glory to him forever! Amen."*
> *(Rom 11:36)*

And so since all things are created *by* the Lord for his glory, we shout Amen! -*"For all of God's promises have been fulfilled in Christ with a resounding "Yes!" And through Christ, our "Amen" (which means "Yes") ascends to God for his glory."* (2 Cor 1:20). The word 'Amen' is usually uttered at the end of a prayer, meaning, 'so be it', an Abrahamic declaration of affirmation (Deut 27:20). 'Amen' is also another name of our Lord Jesus Christ. We see this when Jesus rebuked the church in Laodicea for their spiritual indifferences and compromises, calling them lukewarm in their faith. *"Write this letter to the angel of the church in Laodicea. This is the message from the one who is the Amen—the faithful and true witness, the beginning of God's new creation:"*(Rev 3:14). And so, we rejoice in our Amen by shouting 'Amen!', because his word is true, and his word is good. We worship the Lord this way-*"For God is Spirit, so those who worship him must worship in spirit and in truth."* (John 4:24).

> *"Come, let us worship and bow down.*
> *Let us kneel before the* LORD *our maker."*
>
> (Ps 95:6)

*"The faithful love of the Lord never ends!
His mercies never cease.
Great is his faithfulness;
his mercies begin afresh each morning."*

-Lamentations 3: 22-23

Chapter 10
NEW BEGINNING

JEHOVAH SHALOM IS THE Hebrew name for God meaning "The Lord is my peace" taken from the book of Judges, and first used by Gideon when the angel of the Lord appeared to him in Ophrah— *"Gideon built an altar to the LORD there and named it Yahweh-Shalom"* (Judg 6:24). This had taken place after Joshua led the tribes of Israel into the Promised Land calling them to be faithful to their covenant by obeying the commands of the Torah, so that they would truly represent Yahweh to all their surrounding nations. But

Israel kept failing at this when their judges governed them with corruption before any kings were ever appointed. The book therefore tells a sobering tale of the human condition, and the ultimate need for God's grace to send a king who would rescue his people from the Midianites, as Israel had now developed severe apostasy. This was when they'd just moved alongside the Canaanites and began adopting all their cultural and religious practises, with a series of cycles moving a in a downward spiral of sin, oppression, repentance, deliverance and ultimate peace, pretty much a cycle that most us as Christians go through today.

Gideon began relatively well as a leader, as opposed to the other judges in the book, but might have shown the greatest fear when he experienced his first encounter with the Lord. It's interesting how he's often referred to as 'a mighty man of valour', when really he'd really just shown a great sense of unbelief in the beginning. He seemed somewhat of a weakling who'd always have to validate the Lord's voice. He always needed a sign to prove that it really *was* the Lord speaking, much like Thomas in John 21. So Gideon decided to quickly go and prepare an offering to the Lord-"*When Gideon realized that it was the angel of the Lord, he cried out, "Oh, Sovereign Lord, I'm doomed! I have seen the angel of the Lord face to face!"* (Judg 6:22). This really shook the mighty man of valour when the angel of the Lord suddenly vanished in front of him—*"It is all right," the Lord replied. "Do not be afraid. You will not die."* (Judg 6:23).

Like Moses and Jeremiah, who had excuses about God's calling on their lives, God always reassured his people that his presence would be with them, for He remains to be *Jehovah Shammah*. And this fills us with a great sense of peace, to know that Yahweh is with us, that He is our peace wherever we go because of his Holy Spirit that He has sent into our hearts. Jesus said the same thing to his disciples, "*I am leaving you with a gift—peace of mind and heart. And the peace I give is a gift the world cannot give. So don't be troubled or afraid.*" (John 14:27).

This memory verse, Lam 3:22-23 written by the Prophet Jeremiah, is extracted from a funeral poem of the city of Jerusalem

New Beginning

around 586 BC, an event that happened quite like America's 9/11 terrorist attacks. However, for the nation of Israel, thousands and thousands of people were slaughtered by the sword, the temple was burnt to ashes, sickness and disease ran rampant, and famine got so intensified that some even turned to cannibalism. This is of course much worse than what we see happening today with the COVID-19 pandemic.

Jeremiah recorded five laments for his people to describe the pain and agony that he had witnessed in the destruction of Jerusalem, but amidst all this, he remained hopeful. This verse has long since been popularized and sung in many churches today. The hymn was first written by Thomas Chisholm in 1923, who wrote many poems and music. Chisholm suffered ill health for most of adult life but saw God in the midst of his sickness having had a very low income, and said, "*God has given me many wonderful displays of his providing care, which have filled me with astonishing gratefulness.*" With this in mind, he wrote the lyrics to the song, *Great is Thy Faithfulness* in a letter William Runyan, who wrote a musical setting.

> *"The faithful love of the Lord never ends!"*
> *(Lam 3:22)*

The first part of this memory verse is a reminder about God's faithful love. The prophet had a revelation about God's love, not only typically as Him being a God of love, but also that his love is faithful and unending—"*Understand, therefore, that the Lord your God is indeed God. He is the faithful God who keeps his covenant for a thousand generations and lavishes his unfailing love on those who love him and obey his commands.*" (Deut 7:9). And like the nation of Israel, who were set apart as God's holy people, we are now *also* called God's people. We've been adopted into his family, chosen by God out of his mercy to live as his people—"*For we are God's masterpiece. He has created us anew in Christ Jesus, so we can do the good things he planned for us long ago.*" (Eph 2:10). We understand that God's unfailing love for Israel applies to us too, his children through faith—"*Even before he made the world, God loved us and chose us in Christ to be holy and without fault in his eyes.*" (Eph 1:4).

This in itself should be motivation for total obedience, knowing that we believe that God *really* loves us and that we should surrender our all to this unconditional love we have received by his grace—*"And I am convinced that nothing can ever separate us from God's love. Neither death nor life, neither angels nor demons, neither our fears for today nor our worries about tomorrow—not even the powers of hell can separate us from God's love. No power in the sky above or in the earth below—indeed, nothing in all creation will ever be able to separate us from the love of God that is revealed in Christ Jesus our Lord.*" (Rom 8:38-39).

And so with this in mind, we understand that we have God's peace in our hearts and this is our sure inheritance. Therefore, in all the trials, sorrows and afflictions we face, we are reminded by Jesus that we should take heart and have peace in him (John 16:33). This is how the Lord proves to be faithful, the same words given to Gideon ring out to us in this present day; the very same promises that the people of old relied on, still apply in today's pandemic. This is why we can confidently look back to all the stories in the Old Testament because we understand that God remains faithful, the same now as He was in the past- "*These things happened to them as examples for us. They were written down to warn us who live at the end of the age.*" (1 Cor 10:11).

Therefore God's peace should never be regarded as the absence of fear, or a pandemic for that matter, because often times these events are inevitable. The peace of God comes with knowing that his presence will remain in the midst of the storm. It is his presence in the middle of a pandemic that gives us a blessed assurance of inner peace. And this peace is a virtue that we earnestly need to search for, especially in this era of constant bombardment from social media about threats and trending hash tags of doom and gloom seditions, hatred, racism and insurrections.

The Prophet Isaiah reminds us to fear the Lord instead of fearing what's going on around us—"*Don't call everything a conspiracy, like they do, and don't live in dread of what frightens them. Make the Lord of Heaven's Armies holy in your life. He is the one you should fear."* (Isa 8:12–13). And the best way to intentionally seek for the Lord's perfect peace in the midst of chaos is to be in line with his Spirit, to soak in his presence and give Him first place in our hearts, our lives, our plans, and to continually be mindful of his leading—*"For all who are led by the Spirit of God are children of God."* (Rom 8:14).

The Apostle Paul who struggled grievously with sin in his life reminds us how we ought to eliminate these distractions-*"So letting your sinful nature control your mind leads to death. But letting the Spirit control your mind leads to life and peace."* (Rom 8:6). Struggling with sin for Paul did not in any way make him a terrible person, but a perfect example of a human being who went through the same walk of faith that we are all experiencing in Christ. He's probably one of the best examples of an honest Christian in the Bible, one who was never ashamed to share his real human experience of his faith. We see that he was very well aware of the temptations that the world offers that end up taking our peace away. This is because he'd faced the same temptations himself during his ministry—*"Don't copy the behavior and customs of this world, but let God transform you into a new person by changing the way you think. Then you will learn to know God's will for you, which is good and pleasing."* (Rom 12:2). We therefore need to purposefully balance our thoughts with the truth of the Gospel and protect our innocence. Jesus put it this way, *"I tell you the truth, unless you turn from your sins and become like little children, you will never get into the Kingdom of Heaven."* (Matt 18:3).

It is possible for a believer to have a changed heart. And of course we all do, once we make the Prayer of Salvation following the biblical protocol—*"If you openly declare that Jesus is Lord and believe in your heart that God raised him from the dead, you will be saved."* (Rom 9:10). And so the heart does not become an issue for the lifestyle choices we as believers make. Once there is a change of heart, our names are automatically registered in heaven, in the Lamb's book of Life and we receive the promised seal of the Spirit to mark us as God's own children, a wonderful guarantee to everlasting life. So there is certainly no question about our eternal fate-"*And now you Gentiles have also heard the truth, the Good News that God saves you. And when you believed in Christ, he identified you as his own by giving you the Holy Spirit, whom he promised long ago.*" (Eph 1:13). However, the problem lies between our two ears, our internal thoughts, and how we so often allow them to shape our values and decisions. These either draw us closer, or draw us away from our heavenly Father. And so the choice is ours to filter out the garbage that does not lead us into a restful state of trusting in God—"*Keep watch and pray, so that you will not give in to temptation. For the spirit is willing, but the body is weak!*" (Matt 26:41).

"His mercies never cease."
(Lam 3:22)

Jeremiah, better known as the weeping prophet, often mourned for his people—the nation of Israel because of their anticipated fate that the Lord had revealed to him—"*I am the one who has seen the afflictions that come from the rod of the Lord's anger. He has led me into darkness, shutting out all light. He has turned his hand against me again and again, all day long.*" (Lam 3:1-3). In the book of Lamentations, Jeremiah reveals the destruction of Jerusalem as prophesied in his previous book. He also reveals the second temple built by King Solomon, the scattering of the nation of Israel and their subsequent captivity in the land of Babylon. In a nutshell, the story is about the Lord dealing with the sins of Israel by sending them off to exile to be punished by the Babylonians, while He dealt with the sins of those who remained behind by utterly destroying that remnant that refused to repent.

In this last memory verse, the Prophet Jeremiah had witnessed one of the biggest falls of the nation of Israel, and it makes one wonder, why a prophet who'd gone through such intense torture of seeing his own people being destroyed, having been imprisoned, kidnapped and thrown into a dungeon for several days with no food or water, would get this revelation about God's unfailing love and mercy? This is the very same prophet who wept about the condition of sin that had penetrated the leaders of Israel, which caused the whole nation to stumble and fall beyond repair, saying, *"Is there no medicine in Gilead? Is there no physician there? Why is there no healing for the wounds of my people?"* (Jer 8:22). He really did all that he could to save his people, but all he got was lemons being thrown right in his face . . . worse yet, by his own people from Anathoth, his countrymen.

Well, it probably seems that the prophet knew all about God's unceasing mercies because he had spent ample time in his presence. Jeremiah had a friendship with Yahweh, and knew that at the end of it all, God's word always proves to be true. Paul attested to this truth many years later—*"If we are unfaithful, he remains faithful, for he cannot deny who he is."* (2 Tim 2:13).

"Great is his faithfulness . . . "
(Lam 3:23)

Simply put, mercy can be defined as compassion or forgiveness shown towards someone who has done wrong. This is holding back punishment or judgment to someone who deserves it. It's almost like choosing to erase their record of sin, much like what God has done for those He chose to save—*"So you see, God chooses to show mercy to some, and he chooses to harden the hearts of others so they refuse to listen"* (Rom 9:18). Mercy is how God revealed his love for us, through the blood of his Son Jesus that covers all our sin, shame and failures—*"For the Lord your God is living among you. He is a mighty savior. He will take delight in you with gladness. With his love, he will calm all your fears. He will rejoice over you with joyful songs."* (Zeph 3:17). For this reason, we see that God's faithfulness is indeed great. When we think back to how God found us, reached out to us and gave us new life, that is, when He saved us, we are reminded of how guilty we were of sin. Of course, we all have a different testimony of how filthy and corrupt our lives used to be before we came to know Christ, but nonetheless we can all attest that we were right in the depths of hell. But we know that Jesus is the author of our salvation and He has saved us, and continues to save to this day -*"In this way, God qualified him as a perfect High Priest, and he became the source of eternal salvation for all those who obey him."* (Heb 5:9).

And so for us to come to this knowledge of Christ's death on the cross for our sins, it required God's divine mercy to open up our eyes so that we could see the reality of the ospel of Jesus Christ. This was because of his love for us—*"We know how much God loves us, and we have put our trust in his love. God is love, and all who live in love live in God, and God lives in them."* (1 John 4:16). When the Lord placed his Spirit into our hearts, revealing himself to each of us, this was not because of our choice or internal opinion based on human reasoning. When the Lord laid his eyes on us, it was merely because of his mercy and grace, his free unmerited kindness towards us, that is why He says, *"Now you are my friends, since I have told you everything the Father told me. You didn't choose me. I chose you. I appointed you to go and produce lasting fruit, so that the Father will give you whatever you ask for, using my name."* (John 15:16).

In this regard, we see that God's mercy which is so rich and great compels us to also show mercy to others because we are bound by this law of his love—*"No, O people, the Lord has told you what is good, and this is what he requires of you: to do what is right, to love mercy, and to walk humbly with your God."* (Mic 6:8). Our faithfulness may be meager compared to the Lord's because we often fall short to this glorious standard of showing mercy to others. We are often quick to judge, quick to hold a grudge, quick to pay back and quote this proverb, *"Anyone who injures another person must be dealt with according to the injury inflicted— a fracture for a fracture, an eye for an eye, a tooth for a tooth. Whatever anyone does to injure another person must be paid back in kind.* (Lev 24:19–20). It is sad that we are quick to forget the Lord's great mercy shown to *us* when he chose to save us and forgive us of all *our* sins. In Matthew's account of the beatitudes during the Lord's Sermon on the Mount, he recounted eight blessings of which we should always bear in mind as believers because these are more like the general principles of how things work in the Kingdom of God, and could be compared to the blessings and curses we read about in Deuteronomy under the Old Covenant. One of them has to do with the blessing of showing mercy to others—*"God blesses those who are merciful, for they will be shown mercy."* (Matt 5:7). This is how we ought to treat one another as brothers and sisters, to reveal the Father's love to one another, and to the rest of the world—*"I want you to show love, not offer sacrifices. I want you to know me more than I want burnt offerings."* (Hos 6:6). Jesus wanted us to understand the meaning behind this verse.

> *". . . his mercies begin afresh each morning."*
> *(Lam 3:23)*

In the Old Testament we are told about two amazing prophets who performed great miracles in their time. Elijah, who never died a natural human death but was taken up to heaven by chariots of fire, imparted a double portion of his spirit to his protégé, Elisha who later went on to perform twice as many miracles as Elijah— *"As they were walking along and talking, suddenly a chariot of fire appeared, drawn by horses of fire. It drove between the two men, separating them, and Elijah was carried by a whirlwind into heaven."* (2 Kgs 2:11). Second Kings 3–5 tells of seven miracles that Elisha performed, one of them being the healing of Naaman's leprosy.

Naaman was the captain of the army of Aram, a great and highly respected, valiant warrior, who became a leper. All he had to do to receive healing was follow the instruction of Elisha—*"But Elisha sent a messenger out to him with this message: "Go and wash yourself seven times in the Jordan River. Then your skin will be restored, and you will be healed of your leprosy."* (2 Kgs 5:10). But because of his hardened heart, he thought this wasn't good enough, especially with all the gold and silver he took along with him as an offering. He doubted the power of God and turned away in rage. But by the God's grace, he changed his mind after having consulted his officers who convinced him to try again- *"So Naaman went down to the Jordan River and dipped himself seven times, as the man of God had instructed him. And his skin became as healthy as the skin of a young child, and he was healed!"* (2 Kgs 5:14).

Sometimes all it takes to be healed is to follow a simple instruction from a friend, advisor, a counselor, mentor, teacher, neighbor, spouse, parent, granny, pastor, and best of all, God himself who speaks into our hearts—*"Jesus replied, "I assure you, no one can enter the Kingdom of God without being born of water and the Spirit. Humans can reproduce only human life, but the Holy Spirit gives birth to spiritual life."* (John 3:5-6). And after all, Jesus Christ is our great physician—*"Jesus traveled throughout the region of Galilee, teaching in the synagogues and announcing the Good News about the Kingdom. And he healed every kind of disease and illness."* (Matt 4:23). And so we look to him as our hope, joy and our delight -*"So let us come boldly to the throne of our gracious God. There we will receive his mercy, and we will find grace to help us when we need it most"* (Heb 4:16), because we can always rest assured that everything will be alright—*"And we know that God causes everything to work together for the good of those who love God and are called according to his purpose for them."* (Rom 8:28).

And while we wait for the Lord to act, let's encourage one other with kind words to heal and soothe a bruised soul, being filled with the Holy Spirit—" . . . *singing psalms and hymns and spiritual songs among yourselves, and making music to the Lord in your hearts. And give thanks for everything to God the Father in the name of our Lord Jesus Christ."* (Eph 5:19-20). One of my personal favourites is a song written by Elevation Worship and Maverick City —*Wait On You*. This song should remind us of a wonderful promise in Isa 40:31, that those who trust in the Lord will find new strength. With this in mind, I pray that your trust in the Lord will be strengthened this season.

Take care and God bless.

"The LORD says, "I will guide you along the best pathway for your life.
I will advise you and watch over you."

(PSALM 32:8)

Bibliography

Barclay. "William Barclay's Daily Bible study In The Triumph Of Christ (2 Corinthians 2:12-17)" https://www.primobibleverses.com/commentary/search/william-barclay/47/2/14

Charles H. "Spurgeon's Treasury of David." Psalm 23 Bible Commentary https://www.christianity.com/bible/commentary/charles-spurgeon/psalm/23

Guzik, David. Enduring Word Bible Commentary https://enduringword.com/

———. "Psalm 23—The Lord Is My Shepherd and My Host." Enduring Word Bible Commentary. https://enduringword.com/bible-commentary/psalm-23/.

———. "Revelation 2—Jesus' Letters to the Churches." Enduring Word Bible Commentary. https://enduringword.com/bible-commentary/revelation-2/.

Flight, C. "Smallpox: Eradicating the Scourge" BBC History. https://www.bbc.co.uk/history/british/empire_seapower/smallpox_01.shtml 17-02-2011

MacWelch T. "Survival skills: how to make a torch." https://www.outdoorlife.com/blogs/survivalist/2011/11/survival-skills-how-make-torch/ published 2 Nov 2011

Panchal N et al. "The implications of COVID-19 for mental health and substance use." Kaiser family foundation. 2020 Apr 21;21.

Shipman, P.L. "The Bright Side of the Black Death." 2014. American Scientist. Vol 102. No. 6 Pg 410

Staff. "Global Survey Finds Significant COVID-19 Vaccine Hesistancy." https://www.uspharmacist.com/ 5 Nov 2020

Than. K. "Two of History's Deadliest Plagues Were Linked, With Implications for Another Outbreak." National Geographic Society. https://www.nationalgeographic.com/animals/article/140129-justinian-plague-black-death-bacteria-bubonic-pandemic Published January 31 2014

Wharton E. "Vesalius in Zante" 1902-11-01, North American Review edition, in English.

www.ingramcontent.com/pod-product-compliance
Lightning Source LLC
Chambersburg PA
CBHW070504100426
42743CB00010B/1757